The
Future Healer

The

Future Healer

Spirit Communication on Healing

Ronald Henry
with Kevin Ryerson

iUniverse, Inc.
New York Lincoln Shanghai

The Future Healer
Spirit Communication on Healing

iUniverse books may be ordered through booksellers or by contacting:

iUniverse
2021 Pine Lake Road, Suite 100
Lincoln, NE 68512
www.iuniverse.com
1-800-Authors (1-800-288-4677)

ISBN-13: 978-0-595-40825-2 (pbk)
ISBN-13: 978-0-595-67839-6 (cloth)
ISBN-13: 978-0-595-85188-1 (ebk)
ISBN-10: 0-595-40825-7 (pbk)
ISBN-10: 0-595-67839-4 (cloth)
ISBN-10: 0-595-85188-6 (ebk)

Printed in the United States of America

Ron Henry DC ND FIAMA
Kevin Ryerson, Expert Intuitive

*This book is dedicated to
Those who are guiding us
From darkness to Light.*

Contents

Photos and Sketches

Acknowledgments

I wish to thank my early instructors, who tutored me in my training of physical techniques of healing, and to whom I owe not only knowledge but ethical values as well. They taught me that at the very least, the physician, in possession of the trust of their patients, should follow the Hippocratic oath that states, "Above all, do no harm." I offer my warm thanks to Orville Ladd, DC ND, who instructed me in kinesiology and first made me aware of the meridian system; to Richard Stober, DC ND, who taught me techniques of moving the cranial bones, and to Ravindra Sahni, DC ND, who, by introducing me to homeopathy, sparked my interest in vibrational medicine.

My thanks to MJ Mauro and Rhonda Akin for their initial editing work, and to the medical illustrator Robin Dorn and computer illustrator Jessica Xavier for their artwork presented in this volume and on the book cover.

My special appreciation goes to my dear wife, Natasha, whose devotion and editorial skills gradually refined this book into its present form.

And finally, I offer my gratitude to those who choose to walk by my side in spirit, for without them I would never have made the choice, nor had the material, to write this book.

Introduction

For over twenty-five years Kevin Ryerson and I have been putting our efforts together to come up with the contents of this book. We offer the following material as an attempt to share the remarkable information revealed through a series of channelings with Kevin, who can literally be called a new Edgar Cayce[1]. This information includes enlightened concepts of energy healing, rejuvenation and consciousness-developing technologies, along with excursions into our planet's past, leading to a better understanding of the present.

The Future Healer, which originally started as a personal story, gradually expanded into a much larger concept of planetary healing, where many of us, regardless of our walks in life, contribute to this evolutionary process. Since the beginning of the work with Kevin in 1981, I have believed that one day the recorded channelings would see daylight, and possibly serve as a source of inspiration to those ready for personal change.

From the age of eighteen, when I began having my first spiritual experiences, until now, almost forty years later, I have always been aware of a purpose extending beyond the goals of my own personal life. After following my spiritual teacher, first to India in 1971, and then to many other places across the globe for almost a decade, I have felt that my limited perspective dramatically expanded, awakening my heart to new levels of compassion.

Unable to find the answers from a purely materialistic point of view, I sought to understand what invisible forces could be contributing to our existence. I explored fasting and living foods, studied karate, practiced and taught yoga and meditation, all as a means for expanding my awareness and becoming a more conscious being living a more conscious life. Gradually, the practice of deep meditation, along with life experience, unfolded in me a perspective on the inner workings of spirit that helped me shape my direction in life.

In 1979 I graduated from Western States Chiropractic College where I also completed a special internship with three distinguished doctors who held dual licenses as chiropractors and naturopaths, each with over thirty years of experience. Having expanded my knowledge in *chiropractic*[2], *homeopathy*, nutrition and herbal medicine, I began practicing in Boulder, Colorado in 1980, receiving the Naturopathic Doctor Degree eight years later and eventually completing my *acupuncture* studies at the International Academy of Medical Acupuncture.

I have been running a successful integrated natural health clinic for over twenty-five years, gradually integrating physical and energetic forms of treatment. During this time the spirit guides have been continuously giving me valuable insights into the ethereal nature of matter and ways of utilizing this knowledge in healing.

The twelve channelings included in this book are part of a broad collection of more than fifty channeled sessions recorded during a span of twenty-five years at different locations all over the United States. These twelve channelings, with a few exceptions, took place over three years, from 1981 to 1983-years before Kevin became well known through Shirley MacLaine's book *Out on a Limb*, published in 1983, and the subsequent release of the movie by the same name in 1987. Kevin, whose channeling abilities opened up spontaneously years before our first meeting, is well-known today in the field of parapsychology as an author, lecturer, *expert-intuitive* and *trance channel*, in the tradition of Edgar Cayce. He authored *Spirit Communication: The Souls Path*, described by Shirley MacLaine as "the clearest and most comprehensive book on the phenomenon of channeling," and also contributed to the books *Psychoimmunity—Key to the Healing Process*, by Jason Serinus, *Spiritual Nutrition* by Gabriel Cousens, MD, and *Channeling: The Intuitive Connection* by William Kautz.

Kevin's work, comprising thirty years of exploring intuition, past lives, altered states of consciousness, *futurism* and other relevant issues, is also featured in various magazines such as *Body, Mind and Spirit, US Magazine, Here's Health, Kindred Spirit, English Journal,* etc. He has been a frequent guest on television and radio shows, including Oprah Winfrey, Good Morning America, CNN's Crossfire, Joan Rivers and Tom Snyder. Currently Kevin, whose life work is dedicated to bridging the gap between science and spirituality, maintains a consulting practice in San Francisco, California, providing experiences that touch and change people's lives.

Going back into the past, it had been in the early 1980's when I had first scheduled a meeting with Kevin to gather information about energy healing and the construction of the *pyramidal device*. At the time of that first meeting I had already graduated from chiropractic school and had begun my practice. Surprisingly, while treating patients, I had started developing an ability to receive a clear stream of insights into their physical and emotional conditions.

This unusual experience made me think that I was in contact with *spirit guides* who were helping me diagnose and treat my patients, and were also guiding me in the *pyramid*[3] construction. However, despite the growing evidence, I was still doubtful about the information I believed I was receiving. To my relief, the very first meeting with Kevin had greatly helped in proving the reality of what was happening. I had learned that indeed there were non-physical teachers guiding me in my life's work. Among these guides were Atun-Re, whose last lifetime had been in Egypt several thousand years ago; John, the Disciple, who was also a major spirit guide that spoke through Edgar Cayce; Tom, an Irishman in his last life, as well as an energy healer back in *Atlantis*; and two amazing beings that I had simply come to know as *Deva* and *the Friend*.

Throughout many years of communication with these ethereal beings, I had gradually found myself thinking of them as old friends, feeling at the same time a powerful and tangible connection with them as an ever-present spirit.

As a healer, I have been guided to understand how our subtle nature manifests, layer by layer, through the various energetic bodies, and how these *subtle anatomies* affect our physical and emotional states. What's more, I have had the opportunity to integrate this information into my practice for many years and, most importantly, to observe the results that speak for themselves.

Better understanding of our ethereal nature has also motivated me to explore various forms of natural healing, which compliment each other in restoring health. I am glad that practices such as intuitive energy healing, acupuncture, chiropractic, homeopathy, Chinese herbs, nutrition and many other various energetic therapeutic techniques are finally getting accepted in the field of healthcare, and that many progressive practitioners are successfully utilizing them in their work.

Spirit communication not only gave me many valuable insights into my own healing practice, but also expanded my understanding that this work is only a small contribution towards our collective efforts in the global transformation of consciousness. Many of us are now ready to leave behind any misconceptions about our own nature and to progress to higher levels of self-realization.

This growth in awareness is still lagging behind our technological progress, resulting in wars, depletion of the planet's natural resources, global warming and other consequences of man's inappropriate use of technology. That is why, at this particular time in our planetary history, we are more than ever being attended by the forces of light guiding us in our spiritual evolution, and possibly helping us avoid the mistakes made in Atlantis.

Ethereal technologies hold the potential for our spiritual and physical transformation, through aligning our consciousness with the higher planes. Achieving this state of expanded awareness will result in a society sharing the same ethical values of love and respect towards all manifestations of life on this and other planes of existence. By reducing our attachments to the physical world, we will choose more simple living, naturally conserving our personal and planetary resources. Our need to dominate others will disappear as we learn that free will is everyone's birthright. As we develop our trust in the abundance of life, our desire to serve others and benefit humanity will take precedence over the desire to consume more. And finally, our minds will turn inwards, where the real source of peace and inspiration ultimately dwells.

There is a growing recognition that we, as humanity, are entering the era of more open communication with multi-dimensional consciousness. For those of us who are yearning to expand the borders of our perception, the concepts offered here can reinforce the awareness that such communication is possible and, indeed, is already taking place. It is my hope that this book will help bridge the gap between ethereal and physical realities, and to encourage the knowledge that we are we not alone in our attempts to create a better world.

*   *   *   *

As you, dear reader, explore this manuscript, and especially as you have the opportunity to actually listen[4] to the channelings themselves, certain portions of this work may evoke feelings similar to those that can be awakened by various inspired writings, such as the *Rig Vedas*, the *Dhammapada*, the *Bhagavad-Gita* or the *Tao Te Ching*. Since much of this volume is offered as a *stream of consciousness*, it may hold the potential to produce elevated levels of inner peace and calmness—perhaps even inspiring some degree of personal enlightenment. It is hoped that this might facilitate the achievement of some of the ecstatic states that the author himself occasionally experienced while these channelings were originally taking place. Please remember, life does not move forward in a linear way, nor does this book. *The Future Healer* is about the multi-dimensionality of our existence and the possibility of achieving self-realization, thus shifting into the next phase of our cosmic evolution.

1. Edgar Cayce (1877–1945) is known as "The Sleeping Prophet," because of the trance state he would enter to gain information on subjects such as health, meditation, prayer and past lives.

2. *Chiropractic*—many unfamiliar words and phrases appearing for the first time in this format are defined in the glossary.

3. Pyramid literally means "fire amidst" or "fire in the center of." In the 1970's Patrick Flanagan authored the pioneering work *Pyramid Power*, and also performed much of the original research into pyramids and their effects. He showed that pyramids, because of their mathematical structure and proportion, are able to slow down the ethers and concentrate the life force along their central axis. He was also able to create photographs of this vital energy radiating out of the top, or capstone, of various pyramids, and to measure some of this energy's effects.

4. The recorded audio version of these sessions is freely available at www.futurehealer.com

Part One

Homeworld

In offering these channeled sessions to the reader, I decided not to alter their unique style, but to leave them mainly in their natural form, which can sometimes seem quite unfamiliar. This was to maintain the feeling imparted through each individual session, as well as the integrity of the channeled information itself.

The sessions are placed in chronological order, except for the introductory chapter, "The Prodigal Son," which was actually my last channeled session with Kevin. It is offered as an introduction to give the reader a clear sense of the spirit of the entire channeling section of this book.

The personal stories are also arranged chronologically, although they have no correlation with the channelings themselves. They serve as a background for a better understanding of what has influenced and motivated me in my contacts with the spirit realm.

Ronald Henry, DC ND FIAMA

The Beginning

I lay on my back in pain, looking up at the blue sky through the quivering tree branches. I couldn't breathe—the fall had knocked the wind out of my lungs. I couldn't even call out, for my chest refused to draw in the very air that would let me give voice to my helplessness. I silently called out to God for help, but no reply came.

An overwhelming feeling of loneliness enfolded me. Above me stood the tree I had held myself in just moments before. The blue sky hung quietly overhead, the green grass lay as a soft blanket beneath, but no one was there to help, no God whispered in my ear that I was okay.

It was at this moment of ultimate despair that I concluded I was on my own here on Earth, and that either I was unworthy, or God just wasn't there anyway.

A minute or so later my breath gradually came back and I felt precious air entering my body once again. As I stood up, with tears on my face, still refusing to believe that no one had heard my silent cries for help, no one had come to lift me up and carry me home, and no one had come and made it all okay—I decided, then and there, that we were all on our own.

The years had to pass before this early childhood experience was taken away by a profound realization of our enduring oneness with the divine.

The Prodigal Son

"And he said unto him, Son, thou art ever with me, and all that I have is thine".

~Luke 15

It was May 2006, the time of my latest meeting with Kevin in Portland, Oregon. It had been more than twenty-five years since our first channeling took place, but I had never lost my sense of anticipation and excitement for each upcoming session.

When Kevin greeted me at the door, I again noticed, as I had many times before, his husky build and the pleasant awareness in his eyes. As usual, I immediately felt comfortable in his presence and soon we were ready to continue our journey into the unknown.

In this session I was eager to communicate with one of my spirit guides, named Atun-Re, along with Deva and the Friend—two major sources of inspiration throughout these channelings. I wanted to better understand the spiritual processes that were taking place within me, as well as the possibility of physical regeneration.

The rising flow of the life force throughout my energy channels was gradually leading me into a continuous awareness of spirit, and I was applying this energy to my life's work as a healer. I could feel a growing cycle of inspiration and creativity taking place within my whole being, and an increasing sense of communion with my inner self.

Finally, Kevin turned on a tape recorder and closed his eyes. His body became still and his breathing deepened. In a few moments a deep voice, totally unlike Kevin's, began speaking through. Sitting there listening, I immediately recognized that it was Atun-Re. As soon as the session began I was transported into a realm where time and space had very little meaning.

This channeling happened to be one of the most inspiring sessions I had experienced so far, summarizing our journey as *prodigal sons* and daughters of spirit, who finally come to realize that we have always been divine.

The spirit guides spoke of the re-awakening of our subtle energies, including the *kundalini* force, which would lead to the next stage in our psychic evolution. In this journey of awakening we will be entering more and more into states of *luminous physiology*, as conscious beings of light inhabiting physical bodies. Thus, our physical regeneration will ultimately result from the transformation of our awareness and the restructuring of our subtle energy fields, as we become aligned with universal spirit. As this energy flows through us in the practice of our life's work, we will again find ourselves co-creating with the divine, as we once did in Eden.

*   *   *   *

Atun-Re: Tell us about your experience with the channelings.

Ron: I originally came to Kevin to learn about energy healing and creating consciousness-developing technologies. This has changed my life and now I want to share it with others.

Atun-Re: And how has your life changed?

Ron: In my own past I had aspired to become more than human, and had pursued the goal of enlightenment and liberation. Now, simply being human seems to be divine as well.

Atun-Re: Well, there you are correct. Although you struggle to become an angel, when you actually make it up there and get your wings, all you find is that most angels are trying to scramble to re-enter the birth cycle and become human again. Most angels actually consider it to be a bit boring. They like the variety of being human. That is why it is said that those who know Christ are above the angels. So ultimately it is like a spiritual prodigal son.

You know the story:

The prodigal son leaves home, then squanders his wealth and falls on hard times. But that doesn't mean that the father doesn't send out the servant to find his son and bring him home. Then the inheritance is restored, because the father's wealth is infinite.

But the other inheriting son is jealous, saying, "But father, I have never gone astray." And the father says, "I honor you for that, but we should also celebrate your sibling's return. So I choose to celebrate both of you continuously, because even in your brother's absence I never ceased celebrating him, nor did I ever stop celebrating you."

In a way, angels are like the brother that never went astray, and yet they can still feel some jealousy towards the prodigal son.

Ron: A prodigal son such as myself?

Atun-Re: Yes. Because as the prodigal son, rather than struggling to be divine in another way, it is far better that you become divine in the way in which you already are.

Please continue with your questions.

Ron: These days I feel my own energy systems opening-up and my consciousness expanding. As a result, my own sensitivity to energy fields is also growing.

Atun-Re: And how do you feel your own process of opening?

Ron: My depth of feeling is intensifying. I often feel overwhelmed with love and gratitude.

Atun-Re: What about your sense of communion with your higher self? Are you beginning to receive what you feel are insights and a flow of concepts from that source?

Ron: Yes. In *meditation* I am experiencing increased rushes of what seems to be a kundalini awakening. As I focus my mind inward, my awareness is increasingly drawn within. When I stay focused in this way, more and more energy builds within me, and eventually an explosion starts to happen at the base of my spine. If I continue to stay focused on this force it eventually rushes up and out the top of my head. It is so strong that I feel I can hardly stay rooted in my body.

Atun-Re: Well now, who needs an airplane if the kundalini is awakening? [This comment was a joke about the spirit soaring as one's kundalini opens up. Atun-Re already knew that I was a pilot.]

So in a way these are your first experiences of a new sense of identity. They are the first new waves of your new sense of liberation. Isn't that intriguing?

Ron: Yes. I'm living it and it's beautiful.

Atun-Re: Back in Egypt, students didn't seriously start studying energy fields and consciousness until the ages of forty-five to sixty-five. You are experiencing what was considered in Egypt to be *conscious adulthood*, or *conscious god-realization*. What you are experiencing are the first waves of that awareness.

You are experiencing the next stage of psychic evolution. For instance, while the boney structures of the body become fully stabilized at your Saturn return at twenty-nine years of age, it is in the second cycle of Saturn, that takes place around fifty-eight years of age [I had just turned fifty six at the time], that the neuro-meridian system and the kundalini are developed. The physical counterpart of this process is regeneration, through the awakening of the dormant *stem cells*.[1]

Ron: You mean physical regeneration as a result of psychic evolution?

Atun-Re: Yes. The opening of the kundalini energy, along with the emotional and psychic shifts that you are experiencing, are often the missing links that are required for the regenerative processes to occur.

I believe that you are aware of the work of Robert Becker, MD[2], who has reported on his ability to manipulate mood in response to electro-neuro acupuncture. Similarly, the physician Dean Ornish[3] has demonstrated that to trigger regeneration of the heart and blood vessels an emotional shift must first occur.

Ron: In other words, physical regeneration depends on changes in the subtle energy fields?

Atun-Re: Yes. Expanded consciousness results from the ability to seamlessly integrate the kundalini episodes into the *nadis*, *meridians* and *chakras*. Then, rather than requiring some sort of affliction for healing to occur, the energy that is awakening simply stimulates the next natural evolutionary cycle within the body. You then gradually become conscious that you are a being of energy.

As an example, in the complete astrological zodiac, you have the head and the feet touching together[4], forming a complete circle, and thus bringing together the positive and negative energies. These positive and negative energies also come through the Earth, and on one side they raise the kundalini energy up, and on the other they bring the kundalini down.[5] Do you follow?

Ron: Yes, but where are you going with this?

Atun-Re: When the kundalini energy is awakening and is anchored at the base of the spine, you begin to awaken to the presence of energy fields, and to the presence of other energetic beings that are around you. When that energy then flows through you as an *applied energy* in your life's work [healing for example], you will have created a seamless cycle of energy flow, and will have begun to restore the dignity of yourself as a co-creator with the divine.

For instance, in Egypt, when this energy was used in agriculture, individuals were said to have a "green thumb;" when this energy was used in healing, individuals restored health and wellbeing to the body through transformation of one's consciousness. In fact, back in those days, even warriors worked with the emotions, and understood what effect powerful passions could have on an individual. Because of this, people would even go to them for healing.

In this coming age, genuine healing will consist of balancing the physiological and kundalini forces—thereby creating a being of luminosity. You yourself have already created this in your right labor as a healer, and this energy therefore keeps flowing through you. Another example would be a lawyer transformed by this energy into a poet or diplomat, rather than an argumentative ...

Ron [Interrupting]: I see—it lends a grace to whatever one does.

Atun-Re: That is the whole point.

So in any part of your society, this is what it gifts a person with.

For instance, you yourself have already started moving away from the old bone-cracking phase of your profession, referred to as "carcass throwing" back in Egypt, which is mainly directed towards pain management rather than the raising of consciousness. But in working with energy systems, your intellect also needs an understanding and a confirmation that these new techniques are valid.

For instance, your own intellect is really very interesting. It doesn't originate anything, but it does need to be pacified. To tell you the truth, I always find it a little interesting that one of your own insecurities shows up when you say, "well, I am a scientist," which is a security blanket that your society needs. Actually, all of your great scientists, like Einstein, said that analysis is nothing, and intuition is the only precious thing. Do you follow?

Ron: Yes, and I have a comment. Feeling energy fields, talking to beings that do not have bodies …

Atun-Re [interrupting]: Well, we have *light* bodies … [Joking, but also clarifying the facts.]

Ron: Thank you. And listening to those invisible friends respond.…

Atun-Re: Well, it's not our fault that you are psychically blind. [Joking again, but also offering a perspective on light *beings* from a different angle.]

Ron [laughing]: That's true! And feeling joy as I become aware of the presence of these beings around me. Let's face it, that's not part of our normal earth plane experience.

Atun-Re: It's not part of *your* normal earth plane, but it was a big deal back in Egypt.

Now I am teasing you a little bit here. Believe me, I understand the need for dignity in one's society. I also understand the need for an actual *experience* of this energy in order to move forward in one's work.

In Egypt, when we eventually get you there, we will show you maps of the goddess Newt that depict all the regions of the spine and their corresponding medical organ systems [sounds like modern chiropractic]. So there are actually very ancient maps of this spine-to-organ correlation that are much older than was previously thought. To those of us from [ancient] Egypt we experience a bit of a chuckle that you choose to place so much faith in something that is only one hundred years old called *science*, and in many ways it is more an act of faith than of logical reasoning.

Still, your profession of healing is an honorable discipline. After all, you have two sides to the brain—the *rational* and the *intuitive*. I am merely making the observation that you yourself already do place more faith in your own sense of energy fields than I am pretending to give you credit for. You also practice it fairly boldly, and within the parameters of your own professional discipline [chiropractic and acupuncture].

Our point is that you are already practicing energy medicine, and you are doing so based on your own knowledge and experience of healing. Your awareness of tissue regeneration will continue to increase as you study the works of others who have already documented rejuvenation within the body. You will then recognize what to look for concerning regeneration, and you will begin to intuit when this process is taking place within your patients. It is actually through this seamless integration of observation and intuition that you will experience *true* science. What we are saying here is that your left-brain of logic is starting to catch up with what your right brain of intuition already knows.

A moment here. Are there others that you wish to speak to?

Ron: Yes—Deva and the Friend.

Deva: The discipline of the human tongue in its choice of words must now begin to integrate both the *inspired* word and the *crafted* word. For the inspired word will eventually begin to carry others more deeply into their own true nature than can the crafted word, which only sustains the false dignity that society may bestow.

Thus, the more poetic word, the more divine word, may indeed restore a dignity that may only be transferred and given to the degree that it is able to be received.

There are those who would say the word *integrity*, which is more like the action of a machine, verses those who would say the word *dignity*, which is more so the full measure and value that a person may have in being human.

One can be gifted and graced by the divine only to the degree to which they may also receive. For the limits to which one may receive are to the degree to which their identity may sustain the sacred, and in sustaining the sacred, break not the vessel of their own knowing.

There are those who would use the term *to be brought forth to heal*, but it is more accurate to say that one is *brought forth to be initiated*—initiated into knowledge and wisdom, so that they may come to know the depths of their own true being, that truly was their gift all along. And then if they know any sorrow, it would be that they had not received that gift earlier—not only for themselves, but also so that they could end the sorrows of others. For when one is gifted by the spirit, one feels oneself to be so much a part of the whole that separation of identity, and alones, ceases.

Be at peace with these words and let them inspire and lift thee up, for there is now light, rather than merely the wind, beneath thy wings.

The Friend: I would come and speak so that you may know yourself in a new vibratory capacity, so that you would know yourself in a deeper and more resonant form of luminosity and light. The time has come for the Eden-like restoration of life and awareness upon this plane. For the *flaming sword* [of kundalini] that turns in all manner and in all directions is the key by which one may return to Eden. The time has come where the phenomena to heal will no longer constitute merely the mending of the brokenness of the physical body, but the time has come where one must become more luminous in their awareness upon this plane.

For even as it is known that bone will mend when exposed to simple electromagnetic forces, how much more so will healing occur when the whole of the person is exposed to those divine energies called *prana*, kundalini and the divine energies that flow through the whole of the luminous body and awaken those cells that may indeed bring the person into true rebirth.

For with rebirth you become both male and female, and yet you also become even more than these. For here there is the restoration of the self to the angelic-like state that never left Eden, never left the presence of the throne and never left the presence of the divine. For truly the whole of humanity is the angels which went forth, but turned away too quickly from the divine, in an ambition to co-create with the divine.

The time has now come when your faces turn once again towards the divine, and you know yourselves as luminous beings, and know that all things flow from the divine and return to the divine.

Adonai

After a short pause, Atun-Re spoke again and offered the following information.

Atun-Re: The kundalini, also known as the "flaming sword," awakens the *Tree of Knowledge* as it passes through the chakras. If you really want to know, back in the Garden of Eden, the kundalini was opened up before partaking of the anointment that God was ready to gift humanity with. Through over-eagerness to co-create, mankind unwittingly opened itself to death, and mortality and death have been his concern ever since.

With the opening of the kundalini you gain the awareness of the divine, and you can then be gifted with the *Tree of Life*. The first gift is *longevity*, which allows for an extended life span. The second gift is *conscious mortality*, where you can leave the body as a conscious being of light. The third step might be the extension of your stay in the earth plane, much like a *bodhisattva*. In other words, you would be bordering on what I call *luminous physiology*—physical existence based on a conscious awareness of the *environment of light*.

The *physical* key here is in the triggering of the stem cells that are stored in that unused fatty and connective tissue found within the abdomen. This can lead to a physical transformation where the body is "made new."

If you don't mind we will take our leave now.

John: Hail. Seek to be at peace with these things that are the fruit of thy Father's work, and indeed, ye are that work. Welcome into this thy Father's Light, God bless you. Amen.

Summary

*   As prodigal sons and daughters of spirit, we are on our way to realizing that we have always been divine.

- Conscious adulthood, or conscious god-realization, is our next stage of psychic evolution.

- Development of the neuro-meridian system will lead to physical regeneration through the awakening of the dormant stem cells.

- When kundalini energy starts flowing through us as an applied force in our life's work, it will restore our dignity as co-creators with the divine.

- In this coming age, genuine healing will consist of balancing the physiological forces and kundalini, thereby creating beings of luminosity.

- It is through the integration of both logic and intuition that we will come to experience true science.

- Intuition will become increasingly developed in the healers of the future and throughout every creative aspect of society.

- Genuine healing is an initiation into knowledge and wisdom, revealing the depths of our own true being.

- The opening of the kundalini will lead to a state of luminous physiology—physical existence based on a conscious awareness of the environment of light.

- Our ability to join with the divine will be limited only by our ability to receive from ever-present and all-giving spirit.

1. The big uncertainty now facing medicine is "What are the factors necessary to instruct a stem cell to transform into a specialized cell?" The answer to this question might conceivably allow for the disease-free development, and the complete regeneration of the entire physical body, and thus a state of prolonged life.

    It is likely that the ability for whole-body regeneration and attainment of an ageless state may be beyond the capability of science alone, but may require the union of *intuition and science*, or the merger of spirit with matter.

2. Robert Becker MD, the author of *The Body Electric,* is an expert in the field of biological electricity and regeneration. He is an orthopedic surgeon who has twice been nominated for the Nobel Prize.

3.   Dean Ornish is a well-respected physician who pioneered research into regeneration of the heart. He authored *Reversing Heart Disease, Eat More, Weigh Less* and *Love and Survival.* He founded the non-profit Preventive Medicine Research Institute, and had a one-hour documentary on his work broadcast on *Nova.* He was appointed to the White House Commission on Complementary and Alternative Medicine and was praised by *Life* magazine as one of the 50 most influential members of his generation.

4.   This is a reference to the first sign of the zodiac, Aries, which corresponds to the head, touching the last sign of the zodiac, Pisces, which correlates with the feet.

5.   The Ida and Pingala are the two energy channels to the right and left of the center of the spinal chord that are said to raise and lower the kundalini energy within the spine. These two channels are believed to conduct the essential balancing forces known as Yin and Yang, the expansive and contractive, cooling and warming, masculine and feminine energies of nature.

Discovering the World

I stood on the foot pegs of the bright red mountain motorcycle as I weaved my way through the rocks on the trail. The narrow dirt track leading me through the mossy undergrowth of the alpine forest softly rebounded under my wheels, and the familiar gentle purring of the engine beneath my seat felt like home. The fragrant pine trees stood on each side of the old mining road, offering me shade as I climbed higher and higher towards my destination, the Continental Divide of the Rocky Mountains.

I deeply breathed in the clear mountain air, rich in oxygen from the pine, spruce and fir trees that covered the area, and my excitement continued to grow. Whereas before I could only see strips of green on both sides of the dancing trail ahead of me, now the patches of blue sky became more frequent between the treetops, a sign that I might be reaching the crest of the divide. Another minute or two and a rush of exhilaration burst through me as I found myself at the highest point on the range, where every trail now led down, and only the clear blue sky unfolded above. The great mountain vistas stood before me—huge rocky peaks that rose up into a sky dotted with white billowing clouds lit by a dazzling sun.

I gazed out upon wave after wave of lofty ridges of brown, reddish and green that stood in every direction—motionless monuments to the grandeur of life upon our blue planet. This beautiful globe was my home, and my parent's home and their parents before them, but even at that moment, alone on the top of the Rockies, I knew that there was much more around me than my physical senses could detect. On this very mountaintop I felt that I was on a grand stage extending beyond this world into the unknown, and that someday I would lift the veil and make this unknown a real part of my life.

Years later I realized how precious these teenage experiences of exploring the world were for building my ever-growing sense of freedom in choosing my life path. Looking back, I believe this was also where the spirit of adventure went deep into my heart, leading me to world traveling, car and motorcycle road racing, and flying planes. Above all, these first steps in discovering myself through the prism of the world helped me see my presence on Earth as a great chance to explore both the tangible and intangible forces of life.

1

The Pyramidal Device

"An invasion of armies can be resisted, but not an idea whose time has come".

~Victor Hugo

It was early summer of 1981, the time of my very first meeting with Kevin, who had been invited to give some private channeling sessions in Boulder. I had heard from a friend about Kevin's psychic abilities, and was wondering if he could help me clarify the situation with my own contacts. Although I had been in touch with the invisible guides for about a year by that time, I was still feeling skeptical about the reality of this experience.

I was also hoping to learn more about the building of a pyramidal device [mentioned throughout the book as the *pyramid, device* or *generator*], that could be used for healing—a project I felt guided in by the spirit guides. I had already started designing this pyramid, and was considering buying a three hundred pound crystal to be placed in it.

When I knocked on the door, a pleasant looking man in his thirties appeared in the doorway and, with a smile, reached out his hand, welcoming me in. Before long we felt at ease with each other and ready to start the channeling. At first John[1] came through, and then the Irishman Tom McPherson. Tom's friendly manner of speaking and good sense of humor made him seem very familiar, as if we had known each other for ages [which could be true in this case].

Tom, who, as I discovered later, was a healer back in Atlantis, offered me some guidance on the basic energetic properties of crystals, and the balancing of the chakras and energy fields using the pyramidal device.

During this first session I once again intuitively communicated with a guide that I had already come to call "the Friend." Interestingly, Tom also felt the presence of this being, although the Friend remained in a pure energy state.

Following this session I felt elated. I learned that I wasn't just imagining spirit guides, and that they were indeed supporting me on my path as a healer. Plus, the information Tom shared on the construction of the pyramid encouraged me to continue with the project, feeling the presence of invisible forces assisting me.

*   *   *   *

John: Hail. Question?

Ron: I would like to learn about the healing properties of the crystal that will be a part of the pyramidal device.

Tom McPherson: Tom McPherson here. How are you doing there?

Ron: Fine.

Tom: Excellent. You have come to inquire about crystals, is that correct?

Ron: Yes.

Tom: Very good. I'll tell you what. I believe you have a series of technical questions, and some of my expertise ranges into the area of crystals from my own lifetimes in Atlantis where I used to work with these types of things. I believe that you are to design an owner's manual for crystals, and you also want to build a device.

Ron: A pyramidal device to use the power of crystals for healing.

Tom: I see. This is a very specific crystal, as that will make a difference?

Ron: A three hundred pound, uncut crystal.

Tom: Very good. Three hundred pounds is fairly impressive. I believe I have scouted-out a vibration that appears to meet some such standards. I believe that what you are dealing with here is pure raw power. Crystals have different capacities for broadcast—they have different properties. Crystals have the ability to contain energy. They have the uniqueness of their own energy. They have the ability of amplification. Some of them are better for broadcast in the sense of healing at a distance and some of them deal with pure raw power, perhaps as a storage battery. I believe that you want to attempt to harness this particular device to work in combination with other therapies.

Ron: That is true.

Tom: Now then, in grounding this device, my suggestion is this: the first thing you should do upon obtaining it, or any other crystal for that matter, is to obtain a setting for it. Preferably a setting made from copper. Do you understand that?

Ron: Yes.

Tom: Fascinating, there appears to be a second energy present here. [Tom was tuning in to one of my guides.]

Ron: Yes, I call him the Friend.

Tom: Interesting. I feel their presence. It is rather large and impersonalized, remaining more in an energy state rather than in a personalized form such as I am occupying for communication purposes.

Getting back to the crystal, it is not so much that you are activating the crystal—it is more so that the crystal is activating you.

Ron: Interesting.

Tom: Through meditation, the more energy that is released through the crystal, the more you become bathed in its energy and the more its purifying elements will be working with your physical body. With the help of the pyramid you would be adjusting the attunement of your chakras, which are the seats of your own crystal centers, such as those found in the *pituitary* and *pineal* glands.

Ron: Should the pyramid be made of copper?

Tom: Copper is superior for the structure you are working with. Gold-plating the copper would be superior, as would covering it with silver. The entire dish[2] should be made of copper. The metals that I would suggest for creating such a pyramidal device are copper, stainless steel, gold, and silver. The least useful metal for making pyramids is brass. Stay away from aluminum and iron altogether, as both of these have negative vibrational properties. Remember, there is an entire series of therapies that could be utilized in working with this device.

Ron: Are there any negative aspects involved in doing this work with crystals?

Tom: Only if the individual starts putting too much faith in the crystals and not enough faith in their own healing abilities. Look upon this pyramidal device as an amplifier of your own natural gifts, and decide on the natural gift that you prefer to work with. Eventually, you will probably be working with laying-on of hands, where you will just tune-in to the person. You might also want to experiment with working on the acupuncture points. You may discover that you can get the same types of healing without using the acupuncture needles as you would with the needles by channeling energy through your own hands into the acupuncture points of the patient.

Those are the types of results to look forward to. In other words, everything becomes lighter.

Ron: Can you give me an idea of what the next level of healing is?

Tom: Well, it's pretty hard to top laying-on of hands. I would say the next level of healing is to be able to pass energy directly to individuals, with the pyramid as the source, and the healer as a conductor of that energy.

Ron: Will this pyramidal device allow a reduction and shortening of the healing crisis?

Tom: Yes, particularly as you begin to work with this device knowledgeably. The healing crisis is always less severe if the physical energy flow of the body is clear. If the body is properly adjusted and the *acupuncture meridian* flows are balanced, the process is smoother. For instance, if a person is given a homeopathic remedy, and the physical body is not properly adjusted, the energy released will cause the body to react negatively, because of a blockage in any of the acupuncture meridians, or in the spinal column itself. On the other hand, if the physical spine had been adjusted, or the acupuncture meridians balanced, the energy would have flowed more smoothly.

If there's nothing else we will be going … It's been very pleasant speaking with you and I do hope we have been of aid. Saints be looking after you. God bless you.

John: Hail. Seek to be at peace with those things that you receive in spirit, for you find that they are the fruit of thy Father's works, and indeed ye are that work. Welcome into thy Father's Light, God bless you. Amen.

Summary

- The various properties of crystals make some of them better for amplification and broadcast of energy for healing.

- Exposure to the pyramid will aid the attunement of the chakras, which are the seats of our own crystal centers.

- Through aligning our spiritual centers, the pyramidal device will work as an amplifier of our own natural gifts.

- The next level of energy healing might involve passing energy directly to individuals, with the pyramid as the source and the healer as a conductor of that energy.

- The pyramidal device might allow a reduction and shortening of the healing process, as healing is always more complete when the energy flows of the body are clear.

1. John, one of Kevin's guides, would open and close each of these channeling sessions. Even though John appears only briefly in this book, his presence was felt strongly throughout the meetings with Kevin.

2. There was to be a large metallic dish in the pyramid, which would focus the Earth's energy into the large crystal.

The Mystery of Creation

I suppose it all started when I was about twelve, when we were building the family cabin up in the Rocky Mountains. In the evening, I would pack up my modest two and a half-inch refractor and carry it down into the unwooded valley for a night of stargazing. At that time I didn't know much about the night sky, but the few planets and nebulae I was able to find would captivate my imagination more than any objects on Earth. Considering how unsophisticated my little scope was, most likely no one else would have shared my excitement at the time, but this experience sparked my growing interest in both astronomy and astrology that would extend into the future.

Years later, on a dark and inviting winter night, I stood in my private observatory, its seventeen foot motorized dome turning slowly as I prepared for another evening of viewing. The Milky Way, a vast expanse of billions of suns that collectively look like milk against the backdrop of the dark night sky, hung motionless overhead, nearly spanning from one side of the horizon to the other.

That night I turned the sleek twelve-foot long scope to the Trapezium, a group of four stars that lay in the very heart of the Great Nebula in the constellation of Orion the Hunter, with over three thousand stars in an area covering the size of the full moon.

When I focused the massive eyepiece I was impressed, as always, by both the four brilliant points of light, and the vast array of interstellar dust glowing from the light of these nearby suns, similar to a fluorescent lamp whose gasses are made to glow as an electric current passes through them.

Recently, the Hubble telescope had also photographed *proto-planetary disks* in this sector—dark regions around stars which are the building blocks of new solar systems, each a unique world with its own suns, planets and moons, and whatever else we might discover there in the future.

I gently took in a deep breath as I contemplated the vastness and glory that lay before me. My thoughts wondered around the stars, points of light floating unsupported in the vastness of space, held together by gravity, a mysterious force of attraction found throughout the universe.

Gradually, my attention shifted from the cosmos to the incredible complexity and sophistication of the human system, making me feel that I possibly knew more about space than I did about my own physical form here on Earth.

I pondered upon the energy centers located along the spine, incessantly generating subtle energy fields around our bodies. Do they resemble stars—the vortexes of power radiating their life sustaining force throughout the universe? I thought about the meridians carrying the vital energy throughout the body, and the microcosms of cells communicating with each other through the release of chemicals and infinitesimal transmissions of light.

The beauty and orderliness obviously prevailing throughout the universe seemed to be precisely reflected in the micro-cosmos of our physical bodies, making them a true mystery of creation.

2

Subtle Anatomies

"You are all beings from another realm, pretending to be human."

~Neale Donald Walsch

This channeling took place only two days after my first meeting with Kevin, and was actually an extension of that first one. I was eager to continue my interaction with the spirit guides, who I felt could address many of the questions that had been accumulating in my mind.

In my practice at the office I was becoming increasingly aware that patients' physical symptoms were often, if not always, associated with energetic blockages or disturbances as the underlying source of various problems. Through evaluating a person's energy field, I was increasingly able to associate energy imbalances in their chakras and meridians with specific physical, emotional, mental and spiritual difficulties they were experiencing. The ethereal foundations of disease were steadily becoming my focus, not only for determining ultimate causes of illness, but also as the most reliable means for their alleviation.

In this session, Tom explained the concept of *the ethers* in relation to the pyramidal device, and how the energy of the ethers changes while passing through the crystal. After listing seven different levels of our *subtle bodies*, he outlined the location of seven major spiritual centers along the spine and gave a visualization technique to harmonize them, followed by correlating the chakras to certain organs and glands.

I felt I was being given insights into the connectedness of the whole creation through a universal energy field, which, in turn, allows physical healing to be described in terms of ethereal principals.

*　　　*　　　*　　　*

John: Hail, question?

Ron: I have come again for more information on the crystal. Is a crystal constantly releasing energy?

Tom: Yes, but it is mostly amplifying energy.

Ron: Where does this energy come from?

Tom: Have you heard the theory of the ethers? The ethers are the universal substance. Are you familiar with that concept of physics? The ethers are taken into a crystal, and then their frequencies are temporarily slowed down, similarly to when light passes through a prism and is temporarily slowed down and refracted into its rainbow colors. The energy of the ethers comes through the crystal and is temporarily slowed down to just below light speed, and then radiates out from there.

In addition, the constant steady vibration on the molecular level [within the crystal], known as *Brownian molecular motion,* is constantly producing an energy field. It is not radioactive—it is almost electrical in its nature. It is usually only measurable with the most sensitive of instruments. Such instruments would be those used for measuring the thermo-electrical[1] properties of the body. The thermo-electrical properties could be viewed, for instance, with *Kirlian photography* as well.

Ron: As far as the crystal I will be using, can you give me an indication of the limits of its power?

Tom: Actually, that is a tough question because with pure consciousness almost any crystal has an unlimited capacity. I would say that in using your crystal as a pure energy source for sending energy to individuals, the capacity of this particular crystal is fairly unlimited. As long as individuals are in harmony with the crystal, broadcasting at a distance is virtually limitless. You could reach anywhere on the planet to individuals who are carrying a crystal which has been charged with the pyramid device, and which is therefore in resonance with this crystal.

Ron: My guide would like to talk to you for a moment.

Tom: What do you think he would like to communicate?

Ron: He won't communicate through me. He wants to talk with you directly, in silence for me.

Three minutes of silence.

Tom: Back again. It is very interesting going to a level of pure energy. There is still activity here on this plane, yet the individual I am in communication with remains in a state of pure energy. There is, however, a good possibility that once the device comes to a point of completion, the source that I am now in communication with may choose to personalize himself or herself. There is still some information coming in from this source, but it is coming in on a peculiar level. I would like to continue with a few more inquiries on your part, and then I believe I can relay most of the information.

Ron: In our last session you said you would instruct me regarding the pyramid's effect on the chakras.

Tom: Well, that is a bit of the information that was coming through.

First of all, what this crystal is going to do is to work directly with your subtle anatomies. As you know, there are many different levels of subtle bodies, and many different systems. The systems that we are currently working with here are: the *physical, etheric, emotional, mental, astral, causal* and *spiritual* bodies.

Quite a bit of what the crystal does, in the initial phases, is to work in aligning itself with your etheric body. The etheric body is made up of the substance that lies between the physical and the ethereal. The etheric body is the point where the subtle anatomies translate into the physical. It will be this particular body that will be strengthened first.

However, there is some guidance here from the Friend, as you refer to him, that the crystal may raise havoc with the *astral body* for a while, over-stimulating the dream states. That is why the Friend wishes to first balance the etheric body, which is the closest to the physical. They [the Friend][2] want to ground you first before overexposing you to the crystal's effects. Second, they want to strengthen the emotional body. The mental body they feel is well with you, and if anything, they feel an over-amplification of your mental body.

Above all, what they would like you to do is to take it one step at a time when attempting to approach any forms of application to the causal body. There is a tendency on their part to first strengthen the etheric and emotional bodies, and thus to create more stability and more patience in you as a healer. This will stimulate more empathy between yourself and those to whom the healing is to be applied. There will also be a thickening of the etheric body, which can then be applied to healing.

They would also like you to practice learning to see the *aura* of an individual, and this ability could later be applied in healing. The crystal will have an automatic impact on increasing your ability to see the individual's aura. You will eventually be able to activate your own energy and to touch a person in the area of, for instance, the *medulla oblongata* [at the back of the head] and at the base of the spine, and thus energize their aura to a level where you could see their entire energy field clearly. You'll also be working with broadcasting energy to individuals at a distance.

As you know, the base, or first (grounding) chakra, is located at the bottom of the spine at the coccyx. The second (creative) sexual chakra in a male is found in the testicles, and in a female is found in the ovaries. The third chakra is centered in the abdomen, known as the solar plexus area, and is found in either the spleen or the stomach. The heart chakra is found either in the thymus or the heart itself. The fifth, or throat chakra, is found in the thyroid. The sixth chakra is near the pituitary gland in the forehead, and the seventh, or crown chakra is found in the *pineal gland*, near the crown, or top, of the head.

The Friend wants you to work with a very specific technique with the crystal. Start with focusing on the heart chakra. Spiral down to the solar plexus, then spiral back up to the throat chakra. Spiral back down to the second chakra, then spiral up to the pituitary. Spiral down to the coccyx, then spiral up to the pineal gland. Visualize this as a thin line of energy spiraling to the chakras. This technique would then balance each of the chakras, blending and joining them. There will eventually be a complete therapy for aligning you with the crystal's energy, but this will be the first stage in strengthening both your etheric and emotional bodies in preparation for other works.

I believe that you are grasping this process, although I am a little concerned about what it might do to you. I suggest you just take it one step at a time. There is a little concern about your rambunctious nature. That is why you have been brought into contact with an old, conservative Irishman [a reference to Tom's past life in Ireland], so that you will take these things one step at a time. For instance, the desire you have spoken of to give up all physical medicines and go strictly to purely energy forms of treatment is symbolic of certain levels of impatience and rambunctiousness.

Ron: I have a question, which I am not sure anyone else can answer for me. My feeling has always been to avoid dealing with psychic powers, and now I'm being directed to develop this sort of awareness. I cannot help but feel a certain level of conflict within myself as to whether I should go in this direction.

Tom: You do not enter into the field of the psychic solely to have communication with non-physical beings. You should always rely on your own intuition. To be able to see energy is not so much a development of the psychic faculties as it is an extension of a very ancient form of healing art. These techniques are not for developing the psychic faculties or for reading individuals, such as in past-lives, or clairvoyance. They could, however, be in alignment with your own spiritual processes to be able to see the individual's subtle anatomies, as long as this is grounded out in an intellectual understanding. These techniques then become a science that you are able to apply in a logical manner. It is only the concerns about your own rambunctiousness that cause any real concerns at all.

Ron: My understanding is that there is a certain interaction between all the different levels: ethereal, emotional, mental, etc., and that I'm supposed to align myself with the crystal, which will purify, and then balance, these bodies, with all of this helped along by my practice of meditation.

Tom: Remember, this is an educational process. It was suggested that this would extend over two years, and you must think of it as an occupation. It is a more spiritual form of medicine, in the same way that chiropractic healing is a more spiritual practice than orthodox medicine. However, you already understand the intellectual process of chiropractic healing and therefore do not feel uncomfortable with it. You probably also do not feel uncomfortable when doing *Polarity balancing*,[3] which is similar. What this crystal device will do is take you into a level of seeing the energies directly, and then allow you to apply them in a more exact manner. This is the intellectual level that you are striving to understand.

Ron: I can appreciate that.

Tom: Again, treat it as an intellectual process. It is a project—it is not a religion. You are pioneering into the field of what might be considered *vibrational medicine*. With your knowledge of acupuncture and energy medicine [homeopathy and *Bach Flowers*], the device can be grounded out in intellectual theory and shared with others.

Ron: Is there anything else that the Friend would like to relate?

Tom: He says that the technology that you are building should be looked upon as just that, a technology. It was a technology that was common to the area and place that he comes from.

He would also like to explain one thing. If a patient is ill, and you discover that the illness is being caused by the home environment, and perhaps by the individual's family life, you may choose to take the patient out of that environment and place them in a healthier environment, and their problems may go away. All that is being accomplished in the early phases with this crystal is that the crystal balances the subtle anatomies. The crystal does not alter either the karma or the mental properties of the individual—it just alters the environment of light in which the individual is working. A similar energy principle for promoting health is found in working with *negative ions*.

As you are aware, many persons are already working with energy medicines. It is just that the crystal utilizes a fairly unique technique. It works to heal the subtle anatomies. However, the crystal does not totally penetrate to the causal levels, so therefore, neither destiny nor mental properties are influenced, just the clarity of thought.

Too much exposure to the energy of the crystal would align all of these subtle anatomies a little bit too quickly and would therefore create an environment in which *astral projection*[4] would be much easier. Based on one's own emotional projections and thought-form amplification, the dream state would then become erratic. When one fails to understand the source of dreams, a state of agitation is created in the individual. Without a clear intellectual understanding of this process, an individual might then become superstitious.

Ron: I would also like to know what is this device is tapping into that is not on the Earth.

Tom: Have you ever heard of *The Book of Enoch*? [5] You must think of these things as *points of attunement*. For now, the Friend still wishes to remain in an impersonal state. Most of what you're doing is being too good of a Sherlock Holmes. I believe that you are gaining a mental framework as to where the technology is coming from.

The Friend does not wish to become more personal until you can treat the technology as an isolated phenomenon with which you have complete *free will*. They want you to build a more intellectual basis for the technology, based upon the principles already given.

I am certain that you have your suspicions as to the identity of the Friend. The Friend would like you to go into your own meditations and see if you wish to develop these things as a technology, not as a religion, but as a technology that is based on similar energetic principles such as acupuncture and chiropractic healing.

We must be going now.

Ron: Thank you Tom.

Summary

- The ethers, as a universal energy, can be received and amplified by the crystal.

- The pyramidal device will initially strengthen and align the etheric body, which is the point where the subtle anatomies translate into the physical.

- The crystal will have an automatic impact on a healer's ability to see and work with the aura.

- Strengthening the ethereal and emotional bodies of the healer will give him/her more stability, and thus a greater ability to help others.

- Visualizing a line of energy spiraling through the chakras will be one of the first stages in strengthening both the etheric and emotional bodies.

- To be able to feel energy is not so much a development of the psychic faculties, as an extension of an ancient form of a healing art.

- Ethereal technologies should not be mistaken for a belief system, but considered as a spiritual form of medicine.

- The device does not alter either one's karma or their mental properties—it just enhances the environment of light in which an individual functions.

- The pyramid will create an ethereal environment promoting health and wellbeing, similar to a negative ion generator, which creates a relaxing atmosphere.

1. It is well known that electrical currents travel throughout our nervous system, allowing us to have both motion (through motor nerves) and sensation (through sensory nerves). However, it is less recognized that chemical processes, taking place everywhere in our bodies, also allow for minute electrical currents, which ultimately regulate the smallest units of our bodies, the cells, up to our largest organs and systems. It may be that the health of our physical form ultimately depends on this subtle level of electrical and magnetic forces.

2. Interestingly, in this channeling the Friend is often addressed as "they," reminding us that this refers to a collective form of consciousness, rather than to a pure state of personalization.

3. *Polarity Therapy* is another system of energetic balancing that utilizes energy directed through the hands of the healer or via a magnetic device.

    Whenever there is inflammation in an area of the body, there will typically be the symptoms of heat, redness, swelling, pain and hyperactive function. In addition, there will also be an *accumulation* of sodium ions (Na^+), and thus the build-up of a positive ionic charge (+). This is typically thought of as a *yang*, or overactive, condition in Chinese medicine.

    In the case of an under-active area of the body there will typically be the symptoms of cold, bluish, shrinkage and no pain, but with an eventual reduction of function. There will also be a *loss* of sodium ions, leading to the creation of a negative ionic charge (-), and this is called a *yin* condition. An under-active region of the body will have less energy flowing through it, therefore less blood supply and nutrition coming in to it, but also less blood and lymph flow carrying metabolic wastes away from it. This lack of nutrition in and waste out will lead to the gradual accumulation of metabolic or environmental poisons, which can fester, eventually leading to the destruction of tissues.

    In polarity therapy, the north pole of a magnet, having the same negative (-) charge as the north pole of the Earth, might be used to balance inflamed and positively (+) charged areas of the body. On the other hand, the south magnetic pole, having a positive (+) charge, might affect weakened, negatively (-) charged regions.

4. *Astral projection* is the ability to pass out of the body, either intentionally or unintentionally, and is said to often occur during sleep.

5. *The Keys of Enoch,* by James Hurtak, speaks of opening one's awareness to spiritual transformation and of the education of the soul.

A Search for Meaning

My dream as a child was to design airplanes and build future spaceships, but when I entered college to study engineering I soon discovered that this field was too dull and mechanical to hold my interest. Shortly afterward I quit school and moved with my parents to Texas.

Houston was the place where, at nineteen, I began to study karate and yoga. It happened that there was a new karate master teaching there—a seventh degree black belt from South Korea who had personally trained the Korean national army in hand-to-hand combat, and was one of the true experts in his field. He had also won the Korean National Championships one year, which was quite an honor.

Recognizing an opportunity, I started taking private lessons, and soon found myself spending several hours a day practicing karate. It was one of the hardest physical challenges I had ever undertaken, but as a result, my self-awareness was rapidly growing.

After karate, I would immediately attend a yoga class that same evening. My yoga teacher, a beautiful lady in her sixties, was energetic, kind and intuitive, always finding a way to make her students enjoy every minute of her class. By the end of the evening we would inevitably feel the soothing sensation of peace spreading throughout our bodies and minds.

This first encounter with the balanced disciplines of karate and yoga became one of the factors that defined my decision to return to the University of Colorado, where I had been planning to major in a whole new area of study. By that time I had completely lost interest in what to me was the dry, intellectual field of engineering, and changed my major to psychology, philosophy and religion. There I was hoping to find the answers to the questions perpetually occupying my mind.

Unexpectedly, a couple of months after renewing my studies, my faith in psychology as a way of better understanding the world started changing. I found myself being drawn into an inward search that study in the classroom could not satisfy, and with little hesitation, quit school again. Within a short while I started giving yoga classes and began practicing yoga *asanas* myself as a form of meditation. This intense time of search for meaning finally led me to meeting my spiritual teacher and following him to India.

In the meeting hall of the ashram, sitting with seven hundred other seekers, I heard the speaker, a young woman, telling of her love for God and her devotion for her beloved master.

As I sat there, a strange feeling began to stir within my body and my heart. The floor seemed to start disappearing beneath me, and I had a sense of expanding in every direction. No longer able to tell up from down, or left from right, I succumbed to the waves of pulsating joy that began to course throughout my body, feeling my heart tangibly opening to what could only be described as bliss.

My whole world transformed into an experience of intense gratitude, far more powerful than I could ever possibly imagine—a state of being consumed by a loving, all-engulfing joy and deep appreciation for all of life. The outer world faded away as I sat there in tears, savoring the fulfillment that I had always longed for, and now finally felt. Without doubt, this was the reason I meditated, did yoga, sought teachers, and longed to help others. Now I had my fulfillment, where time and space no longer mattered or even seemed to exist, where all was love.

3

A Message from the Friend

"Let us further come to know ourselves as a reflection of the greater Cosmos and, in so doing, to know ourselves as one with God."

~Malvin Artley, Jr.

It was late 1981 and I was anticipating my third meeting with Kevin, who had come to Boulder again. This was the session in which the Friend spoke through him for the first time.

As I mentioned earlier, even before meeting Kevin, I had already discovered that I was in contact with two spirit guides myself. One was the Friend, the being whose presence Tom had felt during the first channeling, while the other let me know him simply as Deva. Although these beings were directing me in building the pyramidal device as well as in treating patients, so far I knew them only through my own intuitive connection.

The Friend's message presented here was just a small part of a long channeling which took place that day, but I found this to be the essence of what was shared. I clearly realized that the technologies being offered to us are powerful tools for our spiritual transformation.

*   *   *   *

The Friend:

In those times of the technologies which are to come forth and be brought unto you for advancing the consciousness about the planet, that you would take and use these things [technologies] to a higher accord and for the good of all.

That you would graduate into elevating thy own consciousness, and thy own means in their application. But lose not the identity that each of you are as children of God, linked with the infinite. These technologies come at a time when there is a necessity for the rolling back of your own more primitive technologies, so that you may integrate more closely with the type of beings that you truly are, that of energy.

The time has come to end the concept of the self as a physical entity, and to move into the higher *fifth* and *sixth dimensions* that the planet moves into as a whole.

The technologies that are being brought to you, although as a gift, bear the responsibility that you would be fulfilled, as beings of energy and beings of light, as you begin your graduations and initiations as a planet into the higher dimensions.

Adonai

Summary

- The consciousness-advancing technologies being brought to us are to be used responsibly and for the good of all.

- Ethereal technologies will help us integrate more closely with the type of beings we truly are—that of energy.

- The time has come to end the concept of ourselves as mere physical beings, and to move into the higher fifth and sixth dimensions that the planet is moving into as a whole.

Chiropractic School

At the age of twenty-five I had decided that healing would be my life-long work and service. I chose chiropractic as my professional starting point, as I was aware that alignment of the spine brings about powerful releases within the nervous system, leading to alleviation of physical disorders. Chiropractic also offered a convenient way to enter the natural health field, since the licensing for chiropractors allowed them to use a very broad range of holistic therapies besides the adjustment itself. I therefore began intensely studying various systems such as acupuncture, homeopathy, nutrition, herbs, massage, healing touch and magnetic therapy, along with methods for powerful emotional release, one of my favorite techniques being based on the book *Life Energy* by John Diamond, MD.

Now, in my final year of school, I found myself fortunate enough to meet three old-time doctors who were all willing to accept me as an apprentice. Each held great credentials, and was considered by his peers to be among the top in his field. Combined together, they had over one hundred years of experience in the healing arts.

I also had a few interesting experiences while in chiropractic school. I can remember one day strolling down the hallway and passing one of my instructors. He observed me as I was about to go by and saw that I was carrying a rather large briefcase. It must have caught his attention because, looking curious, he asked me: "What are you carrying in there Ron?" I replied that these were my homeopathic remedies and that I was going to use them on my shift at the clinic. Looking somewhat disturbed, he protested: "We are chiropractors. We adjust, we don't give 'drops!'"

I responded that I was interested in discovering *whatever* methods I could that might help my patients, and I have kept this attitude until the present day.

4

Ethereal Healing

"The real voyage of discovery consists not in seeking new landscapes but in having new eyes".

~Marcel Proust

It was early 1982 when I had my fourth channeling with Kevin, which was the first of two related sessions [chapters 4 and 5]. Since our last meeting several months earlier when the Friend had spoken through for the first time, my whole awareness of the non-physical planes had deepened. I had become certain that the Friend and others were some of the most transformational beings associated with our planet, and that it was a remarkable privilege to be guided by them. I was growing in awareness that, along with many others, I was a vehicle for planetary healing and transformation.

My depth of communication with both Deva and the Friend was increasing, and I was waiting for Deva to speak directly through Kevin for the first time in one of the coming sessions. I was realizing that these contacts had a much deeper meaning than merely guiding me in my healing practice. They held the message that our planet, as a whole, was rapidly moving to its next stage of evolution.

In this session I wanted to learn more about ethereal technologies of healing, which I was finding increasingly fascinating. I felt captivated not only by the information itself, but also by the universal consciousness behind it.

In this channeling, the pyramid was described as a psychic *Faraday Cage* that screened out the general thought-forms of the planet, permitting only pure thoughts from Homeworld to be broadcast through it. When our personalities align with these impersonal levels of the causal plane, we move one step further to becoming spiritually realized.

*   *   *   *

Ron: I have come to receive information from Deva and the Friend.

Tom: Tom McPherson here. How are you doing there? Do you have a focus of what you want to ask today?

Ron: Not in particular, but I believe the Friend has a message for me.

Tom [After tuning in to the Friend's energy]: Would you like more information on *the generator*?

Ron: Yes.

Tom [communicating the Friend's message]: You will gradually move away from some of the more physical theories of healing, possibly even from the more radical elements of your own homeopathy, and will begin to work towards more *ethereal* techniques of healing. You will still be working, to a certain degree, with the physical properties of the body, such as in spinal alignment. However, this will only be so that the physical body can receive the necessary healing. The other thing that the Friend wishes to incorporate is that eventually, not only will you be healing and rebuilding physical bodies, but you are actually going to begin gathering to yourself a number of individuals in order to advance the levels of their own consciousness, so that they, also, will become *instructors in light*. In other words, you are possibly going to be rebuilding *new people*.

In the early phases of the work, your healing practice will bring individuals into a state of physical wellbeing. This will reduce their survival instincts by bringing them into a proper state of health. You will initially be applying the basic theories of healing to bring individuals into a more altruistic state—not unlike a yogi who first masters the physical form, and then knows that by mastering the physical form he overcomes the fear of physical passing. The individual will thus immediately be able to be more generous and more open. It is when you have an individual in this more palatable state that there can be the direct alignment of consciousness that the Friend would like to convey to a person: aligning their soul's path with their higher *dharmic works*.

In a way, it will be like a garage for "tuning-up" a certain *soul group*. In other words, individuals will be coming in for physical wellbeing, as well as to be healed upon several levels of their consciousness, and for opening themselves up to their own intuitive abilities. For instance, after aligning many of an individual's chakras, and bringing them into a space of wellbeing on the physical levels through the traditional healing arts, you might then facilitate the alignment of the direct expression of their different levels of consciousness, and they might then work with meditation techniques on their own.

I believe the Friend is going to bring meditation techniques to you that will align individuals with some of their own dharmic works.

Does the Friend have any commentary through your own personal communication just yet?

Ron: Yes, he does. The Friend suggests that you speak about the specific properties of the generator itself, and how it will be used as an instrument for healing the various subtle bodies.

Tom: Oh, he wishes for me to relay that bulk of information?

Ron: Yes.

Tom: You're not speaking of the assemblage of the device, are you?

Ron: No. We're talking about its utilization once it is totally assembled.

Tom: The generator will broadcast an energy that is very unique. It will be an energy that will align consciousness in many individuals, particularly those who have already expunged themselves of energy blockages.

Your purpose here is to create a number of *living crystals*[1] to whom specific information, levels of consciousness, and technologies will be broadcast to. The generator will be the focus of that activity. Their exposure to the series of treatments that you use to clean out their own "internal crystals" will then give them an attunement with an organized body of knowledge, which will then find itself expressed through their individual talents.

One of the generator's purposes is to align information flows and consciousness, and to help spiritualize the talents already inherent in an individual, and then to align them with their ultimate dharmic or spiritually applied state.

What you are dealing with here is personal and spiritual transformation. So what you're doing is engineering a soul group. These are not under the dictates of the Friend—it is just that the device creates an environment where individuals may choose, by their free will, to have an attunement with spirit. Many individuals would naturally feel a magnetic draw to the device as they became involved in this work.

May I now go on to other areas of purpose?

Ron: Yes, specifically on how the generator functions.

Tom: The generator works on several levels. The crystalline structures within the generator have thought-amplifying capabilities. The pyramidal structure built around the crystalline structures acts as the equivalent of a psychic Faraday Cage, filtering out all negative external thought-forms. And since the thoughts to be amplified are those of the Friend and several other angelic hosts, those thoughts are basically divine.

The more typical use of a crystal ball is to meditate on it and see what types of imagery would transpire. In this case, with the Friend aligned with a soul group that is already out there, it is like the equivalent of a "telepathic pep-rally" for that particular soul group. The outer structure of the device would seal-off unprepared thought forms, and the energy, therefore, would be much purer. In the same way that you may go to an individual who is blessed with oratorical skills and become inspired by them, the Friend is working more with direct telepathic exchanges with individuals to raise their consciousness on subtle levels. The energy will then come to them as *pure inspiration.*

It is quite possible that you will be sent a range of individuals whose original intent may have been physical healing, but you will intuitively receive guidance concerning certain treatments that will enhance their awareness. It will be up to your perception as to how much of this information you want to entrust to them, as that will be your test.

Ron: That means the Friend would like to give me a test?

Tom: In many ways, yes.

Other principles on how the device works are the *piezo-electric* effects. These effects of the crystals[2] allow them to amplify thought-forms. The spherical structure of the crystal balls basically stabilizes those thought-forms which are not coming from the *fourth* or fifth dimensions, but more like the sixth and *seventh*, and they need a point of focus here in the earth plane.

Ron: May I have a clarification of what the fourth, fifth, sixth, and seventh dimensions are?

Tom: The fourth dimension, of course, is just the normal time-space continuum and is governed by the laws of physics that your physical universe functions in. The fifth dimension is where the ether fields dwell, and is the driving engine of energy that keeps your universe in a continuous state of expansion, both literally and in consciousness. The fifth dimension is the ethers, but is still part of the "yet to be discovered" laws of physics. The sixth level is even beyond that of the ethers—it is where pure consciousness dwells.

Ron: Are the causal and the astral bodies in the fifth dimension?

Tom: The astral is more of a fourth dimensional phenomena, whereas the causal plane is somewhere along the fifth dimension. The astral planes are found in the curvatures in which you travel in this dimension, and you can still become confused there by random thought forms. It is this particular level of energy of the fourth dimension that the outer structure of the device isolates the crystalline structures from. The fifth level is what charges and powers the device, whereas the sixth level of consciousness is where the thoughts actually come from.

The device aligns the earth plane inspiration on the more personal level of the astral plane with the more impersonal levels of the sixth and seventh dimensions. The astral body is what preserves the more positive aspects of the ego, and preserves the parameters of the personality, i.e. your loves, your desires, your anger, your emotions, your weaknesses, and all those things that make you human.

But it is the causal plane that aligns the person with purpose. It is in the causal plane that an individual becomes a causal being. It is where one is no longer reacting to the earth plane, but is becoming the *law of that plane.*

Finally, when consciousness is integrated with a healthy functioning human personality, the person then becomes the whole individual, the wholly spiritually realized individual.

When he becomes conscious, he then becomes the fully causal and conscious person—the spiritually realized person, within whom the mind, body and spirit are linked in common direction and cause. He then uses his human personality to communicate to others the things with which he is aligned.

Ron: Will you talk about how the generator uses the kundalini energy of the Earth as a power source?

Tom: Well, for one thing, this is the aspect of the generator that works within the fourth dimension, because the kundalini energy of the earth functions within the known time-space continuum. The crystal also aligns itself with the seven chakric points upon the planet. [I had been intuitively informed that, like human beings, the crystal possessed all of the seven chakras.]

The Earth's chakra points are located where humankind experienced different stages of evolutionary consciousness. Have you heard the theory of *multi-dimensional lives?*

Ron: I don't believe so.

Tom: It is the idea that all of your lives are happening simultaneously.

Ron: Well, um, that's interesting.

Tom: When all of your lives are happening simultaneously … Perhaps they go all the way back to *Lemuria.* You would be going all the way back to the very base chakra itself. During that historical time frame the base chakra was an attempt to ground humanity out in the earth plane. When you went on to the second chakra, you were attempting to create things in the earth plane while still being grounded. The third chakra was sensitivity, the heart chakra was balance, and so on.

With the large crystal attuned to all of the Earth's seven chakras, when individuals are brought into exposure to the crystal, and therefore to these different historical points on the planet, the device then aligns the entire ancestry of the past-lives of the individual with their current lifetime.

In the same way, an orphan, who does not have a clear understanding of their parentage or lineage, feels incomplete, and yet when they find out what their history is, whether it is positive or negative makes no difference, they then feel more complete within themselves. So when an individual becomes aligned with the Earth's kundalini energy and the Earth's seven chakras, all his past lives then find themselves in alignment—not necessarily with the literal history of those past-lives, but aligned with their experience relative to those different historical locations on the earth plane. He then becomes totally aligned with his current position and purpose on the earth plane.

Ron: You mean that one may not have a conscious awareness of those past-lives, but will have the essence of what was gained and learned from them as a part of one's present life?

Tom: Absolutely! One of the key things here is that when a person comes into total awareness of his past-lives, he immediately stops caring about them.

Ron: I understand, but I haven't experienced it yet.

Tom: Again, the best psychological model is the orphan. The orphan will hunt and hunt for their origins and family of birth, and has this agony that blocks him from accomplishing anything else, but once he has found it, the past is no longer of such a great concern. It just becomes a part of their being. It would probably increase a person's recall of past lives, but eventually it would no longer be of such a great concern to them.

Also, by aligning oneself with all of the chakras on the planet, it gives one a greater sense of freedom of movement to be able to travel to various locales. For instance, the true yogi can go anywhere and be at home. If a person aligns only with a singular past-life, they will only be attracted to the cultural and architectural activities of that particular time. That is part of what you will be instrumental in creating: *planetary citizens.*

Ron: The Friend also wants you to talk a little about himself.

Tom: First of all, the Friend is basically pure consciousness. He functions very much on the *soul levels.* First you have God, and then you have soul levels. The Friend functions from pure levels of consciousness, and is using the generator as sort of an earth plane focus.

Ron: I have a question. It seems that the higher up in consciousness one goes, the more unlimited the knowledge and abilities become. Why is there a need for anything physical like a pyramid generator?

Tom: For the simple reason that was spoken of before: if one single individual in this soul group were to have too much exposure to the Friend, they would "burn out." I believe this is your term for it. For example, when Saul[3] met Jesus on his way to Tarsus he was basically blinded, and was then led around babbling for a number of days until he was able to assimilate the realization.

Since the Friend wishes to remain as pure consciousness, the pyramid generator is being built for the purpose of giving the Friend a point of focus. But even any one single generator could not focus all the consciousness that is desired. What the Friend is doing here is building an automated sort of device for mind, body and spirit transformation.

The Friend's basic makeup is that of pure consciousness—androgynous, I would say, being neither male nor female. Currently, the Friend is working to uplift the *feminine consciousness* of the earth plane to balance out the overly crystallized masculine aspects of this plane.

Ron: I understand.

Tom: Do you wish me to detail the kundalini energy of the planet?

Ron: Yes, in the sense of how it directly affects an individual as their consciousness is awakened.

Tom: Again, the main sense is freedom—freedom to go anywhere and do anything. This is why the Friend encourages first aligning the proper personalities, and wishes you to be very careful about the personalities that you choose to expose to these energies, except for basic healing.

The first priority is to develop a stable personality, which comes from the fourth dimension. Only then, if they feel aligned, should you initiate them into the deeper mysteries.

An example would be a businessman exposed to a guru, who then sells his business, leaves his family, and trucks off into the Himalayas to live in a cave for the rest of his life—this is not what the Friend desires. What he desires is a balanced approach of first being exposed to the energies for healing the personality, then initiating individuals into the more causal energies, aligning them with the planet's chakras. This will re-kindle within them a sense of freedom, and it will also re-kindle a sense of responsibility— they will want to be responsible with this energy. Then, in the final phase, after they become more causal, they would be initiated into the parameters of their own consciousness.

The key element is in first finding these grounded personalities. If individuals come to you with wild and outrageous personalities, the energies of the device will only magnify their imbalances, unless, of course, you only work with them physically.

The Friend wishes to coordinate several soul groups with their natural levels of work, so that they can become balanced. The energy will merely go out to them as pure inspiration. Individuals will then be dealing more with guidance, inspiration and consciousness, rather than dictation [or specific concepts]. Are there any other questions?

Ron: On a closing note, I just received the communication that the Friend has one more message to convey.

Tom: Oh, you would like me to relay that then? The Friend desires to communicate, basically, love and light, and to always realize that these things are attempts and works with the higher purpose of the Father, whom we are all not under, but are all a part of.

I believe that Deva can speak through more clearly tomorrow, perhaps with more detail.

Summary

- We will gradually move away from the traditional therapeutic practices towards more ethereal techniques of healing.

- When we reach more advanced levels of consciousness we ourselves will become instructors in light, aligning our soul's paths with our higher dharmic works.

- As consciousness is aligned, our intuitive abilities will open, and we will begin to work more with meditation techniques, focusing the mind within the self.

- Cleaning out our own "internal crystals" will give us attunement with an organized body of universal knowledge, spiritualizing our already inherent talents.

- The pyramidal structure built around the crystals acts as the equivalent of a psychic Faraday Cage, filtering out all negative external thought-forms.

- The piezo-electric property of the crystal allows it to stabilize the thought-forms coming from the sixth level of consciousness and beyond.

- The device aligns the personality with the more impersonal levels of the causal plane, giving birth to a causal being—a spiritually realized person, within whom the mind, body and spirit are linked in common direction and cause.

- When we become aligned with the Earth's kundalini energy and seven chakras, all our past lives become aligned as well, allowing us to become totally focused upon our current position and purpose on the earth plane.

- The Friend, who functions on the soul levels, is working to uplift the feminine consciousness of the Earth, to balance out the overly developed masculine aspects of this plane.

- In order to be initiated into the higher dimensions of our own consciousness, we must first develop a stable personality on the earth plane.

1. Due to the ability of certain cells in the human body to transduce energy, they may come to function like crystals, allowing for the free-flow of the life force throughout the physical form. For example, crystal-like structures such as bone display electromagnetic phenomena. Bone is a sophisticated crystal, where 70% of its mineral content is made of minuscule *crystal flakes*, having a strong ability to convert pressure into electric current.

2. Crystals may be tuned to resonate with specific radio frequencies. In fact, some of the original radio sets consisted of a crystal that could be tuned to receive a particular broadcasting station, but had no direct power source of its own. The energy of the radio station's transmitter supplied the power, and the crystal simply resonated to that frequency once it was tuned in. Because there was enough electrical current generated by the vibrating crystal to power a small earphone that went into the listener's ear, the radio did not need a power source of its own. Although more sophisticated in modern times, the same principle still applies today for radio reception and communications.

3. Paul of Tarsus, also known as Saul, or Saint Paul the Apostle.

First Steps in Intuitive Healing

I had just graduated from Chiropractic College at the age of thirty when Dr. George Graff, one of my close college friends, invited me to practice with him in Boulder, offering to share his office with me. There, in my first year of practice, being fresh out of school, I was seeing only two or three patients a day. Little did I know how everything would soon change.

One day George, who was also a pilot, flew off with some friends over a rugged portion of the Rocky Mountains en route to a music concert. Unfortunately, on the way back, a sudden storm kept him and others in the plane from ever making it back alive. This tragedy, in turn, brought big changes into my own life, since I immediately inherited George's full-time practice in Boulder.

By treating a large number of patients, I soon learned that even though the *possibilities* for healing were unlimited, getting to the root of one's problem could be difficult and complex. I felt unprepared for dealing with actual patients in the real world, despite my best attempts to apply all the knowledge I had.

The answer to my quest came one day in the form of a complete surprise. One afternoon, while treating a patient, I experienced receiving a clear stream of insights into diagnosis and methods of treatment, which was like having someone talking inside my head. What's more, along with the new information, this voice seemed to include practically everything that I had learned so far. Wondering if it was my own intuition opening up, as I believed could happen to someone deeply passionate about what they do, I also considered that I might be imagining it all.

Over time, I came to discover an even more amazing ability of this voice to integrate most of my acquired knowledge. The clarity of perception that it gave me was like having an open window into every patient I saw. Indeed, it was my own intuition aided, as I learned, by my spirit guides.

However, I was soon to realize that even intuition, with its seemingly effortless ability to know and to integrate, was not, by itself, perfect. On the contrary, I quickly discovered that I could still make mistakes, both in treating patients and in my personal life. Indeed, I was to learn that my rational abilities were just as important as ever, but now they were working with an ever-increasing and equal partner—the intuitive and integrative side of my consciousness.

5

Technologies of Light

"Any sufficiently advanced technology is indistinguishable from magic".

~Arthur C. Clarke

This session took place in 1982, only a day after the fourth channeling. It was the first time when Deva, who I had been communicating with intuitively, came directly through Kevin. I felt that we, as humanity, were approaching a moment when Deva and other beings of light would share with us a plan for both personal and planetary transformation.

Deva spoke of coming into full *planetary consciousness* where, supported by ethereal technologies, our individual awareness would be united as one. The pyramidal device was described as a *technology of light*, acting as a fourth and fifth dimensional *mandala* and a point for the higher self to meditate upon. It is also an amplifier, able to access the full spectrum of creative thought associated with the earth plane.

Nevertheless, the time will come when our physical bodies will *become* the technology[1] itself, because of the potential of our ethereal nature to align with the Divine. As part of this process, our bodies will gradually produce greater amounts of a substance known as *magnetite,* which will help stabilize our auras and eventually allow for on-going self-regeneration.[2]

I was glad to hear that many of our children have come as carriers of these new ideas, some having a fully functioning eighth chakra through which they have never lost the connection with their higher self.

After hearing Deva speak, I felt ecstatic. By the end of the channeling my heart was wide open, and I knew without doubt that I was ready to serve the forces of light.

*   *   *   *

Ron: I have come hoping to hear from Deva, one of my spirit guides.

Tom: Hello there, how are you doing?

Ron: Not bad, Tom.

Tom: First of all, I believe that Deva can align for a goodly portion of this particular channeling, as I don't think this energy is alien to the alignment with the physical instrument [Kevin's physical body].

I believe that Deva is a single energy force, yet the being moves closely with others, almost in a collective form of consciousness, rather than in a pure state of personalization.

Do you have any specific inquiries, so that I may stall for a bit of time here while the alignment takes place?

Ron: I believe that something specific might be coming from the Friend.

Tom: I believe that the Friend wishes to point out that the technology of the planet has become such that you are now, officially, a society that is manifesting itself through a technological expression. It is not that the nature forces have totally lost the battle, and it is not that you cannot return to an ecologically and *horticulturally* based society, indeed you will. It is just that you have made such strides as a society into technology, that technology has become part of your imagery, and has therefore become one of the major focuses of consciousness on the planet.

To increase the Friend's access to the earth plane, the energies must therefore come through a very specific type of technology—one that is currently the expression of the plane. Therefore, the information is now coming through more of an electronic form of apparatus, such as you are constructing. The information, however, is still based on esoteric and ethereal principals.

Ron: Will the Friend talk a little bit about my son, Deepak? [Deepak was only one year old at the time, but I wanted to know what part his generation would play in the planetary evolution.]

Tom: A key communication here is that this is a soul who has come in at this particular moment in time to be able to assimilate most of these vibrations. The individual will have an excellent opportunity for being one of the first souls to be initiated fully into New Age climates where awareness of spirit will slowly be accepted as a social force, rather than being merely a private religion or superstition.

 This particular soul has come expressly to be one of the carriers of these New Age concepts, above and beyond just a private religious belief, but more-so becoming an actual part of the social practice. He will not be alone in this. There is an entire soul group that has incarnated a few years either side of this particular soul who will be banding together to accomplish these elements. It will be above and beyond just the healing fields. It will begin to penetrate all aspects of the scientific community, and will also transform the various social forces that are shaping the planet. You might call this soul somewhat of a New Age revolutionary. This may be one of the first souls coming into the planet that has a fully functional *eighth chakra*, along with the other seven chakras. By having a fully functioning eighth chakra, an individual is able to maintain a direct link with the higher self. This is a rare phenomenon, but I believe that this particular soul has this capacity.

 Training for this particular soul would involve the imparting of knowledge about the basic ethereal nature of mankind, by making it part of the intellectual studies and pursuits. This soul should be taught this information almost as second nature, rather than as theories or principles. They should be taught on the same factual basis as two and two equals four. This will allow the individual to express, and to develop, their chakra centers more naturally, and to develop them the same way an athlete develops the muscular tissues for a certain game or sport.

 A moment here—I believe that Deva can come through. Would you enjoy that?

Ron: I would love it.

Tom: A moment, please.

Deva:

> *Heerlem Abetoth Selom Sabatak*
> *Amon Elum Selum Elohim Serlom Hala*
> *Alom Selom Elum Elohim Alum*

I come to reveal to you further wisdoms from whence you will bring forth your projections and desires to be balanced within the activities of the earth plane.

You have come to build and bring forth a citizenry of light. You have come to bring individuals into full *planetary consciousness*, so that they will grow and bring forth planetary consciousness through the alignment of their own chakra forces with the alignment of the seven planetary chakra forces, so that they will unite and become as one.

There has been the slow drifting from the natural states of the planet towards imbalance—not holocaust, but perhaps even worse—imbalance within the forces of light upon the planet. These forces of light, seeking to stimulate greater balance and greater understanding, have been brought forth by thyself who shall seek to stimulate new understanding, new consciousness within individuals, creating a soul group, rapidly evolving their evolution. There have come forth upon the planet rapid advancements in man's awareness of his sciences, but there has not been the quickening of the pulse of his consciousness.

Therefore, there has now been introduced upon the plane, through thy attunement, a *technology of light* that may help quicken the pulse of consciousness upon this plane, and by quickening it, balance the forces of light.

These, of course, are the duties and charges of all men and women who have chosen to incarnate upon the physical plane, so as to become totally at one, and stay at one with the planet and its forces. These forces are to come forth in expressions of technologies of light, to come to realize the specific focuses of consciousness: that indeed you, also, are souls, and are at one with the universe. The technologies of light shall be like tapestries woven between individuals, that shall create a network of light between individuals. They shall be scattered to all points of the four corners of the Earth, to bring forth greater and greater light, and greater and greater illumination.

There are many trilogies within trilogies. You have created your device as one axis of a trilogy, in which others are interlinked in same. These shall come forth and find their placements upon the various centers of light upon the planet, and shall continue as outreaches to each other. You may aid others in uplifting their consciousness by first healing them in the physical and making them aware that the physical is indeed divine, for it is the temple wherein the living God dwells.

Then, there shall be the going forth of these individuals to claim consciousness, and with consciousness, purpose. These individuals shall go forth and shall stir up forces in both thy society and thy technology, bending them to the will and the service of God, who is the whole.

These developments shall come about through thy own knowledge—knowledge of healing, thy knowledge of anatomy, but above all, the development of the knowledge of the healing of the individual. For the individual may still have purpose, yet still be part of the whole.

This healing shall come about through the sciences of linking first the seven chakras of the individual with the seven chakras of the planet. This healing process shall come forth by awakening within individuals aspects of consciousness peculiar and unique to them. You in your own right become "living crystals." The alignment of thy own chakras with the seven planetary chakras shall create a sympathetic resonance, whence you may pass through thy own hands the alignment of other chakras, actually molding and sculpting the subtle anatomies, and cleansing them of any imbalances.

The test for individuals shall be their own physical healing—their patience with it. If they pass this simple test in the physical and accept their own healing, then they would be worthy of the higher realms of consciousness that would then flow into them, in this work and in this mission. The testing would be simple: if they align and then accept their own healing, then in turn they gain the authority to pass healing to others, for it is only through experience of one's own healing that individuals gain authority.

This is why you have had your own testing: this is why there has been kindled within thee your own testing, so as to gain authority in these areas. But also the individual must develop the love and the concern for individuals to be present with them in a state of patience, and to communicate to them deeply those things that ye desire for them to feel or to express. These are indeed imparted unto thee.

You shall come into knowledge and more and more expressions. Eventually, there shall be the abandonment of all forms of the physical expression of this technology, and indeed, the individuals shall *become* the technology. They shall become the expression of the instrument you now build. The instrument that you build is but a focus, an image that then may be passed on to others. It is a physical focus to screen out all of that which is negative. It is a symbolic pattern to be in the world, but not of it. It is a three-dimensional and fourth-dimensional mandala. Its patterns are activated not only as a point of focus as two-dimensional mandalas, but its point of focus is also found within the fourth and fifth dimensions and realms of consciousness. It is a mandala that is neither two-dimensional nor even three-dimensional, but fourth and fifth, which may then be meditated upon.

The pyramidal device is a point of focus for the higher self, not for just the conscious self. It is a meditation and a mandala for the higher self, which is not spatially limited to only three dimensions, but which dwells and inhabits on the fourth, the fifth, and the sixth levels of consciousness.

This, then becomes a mandala for the focus of an individual's consciousness, aligning all the past-lives—aligning the individual, so as to draw forth selectively naturally those talents and those properties with which to serve the greater whole.

The higher self would, indeed, become like an eighth chakra, when it comes into total alignment with all the past-lives. This allows the fulfillment of the totality of the self, and the merger of not only mind, body, and spirit, but also the merger of the expressions of consciousness, and the merger also of the conscious, subconscious and super-conscious.

This activation stimulates an individual in becoming the total-self, the complete-being—the being of light that, indeed, all are. And when you become as the being of light, you become like the central sun, which may nourish all about you. All about you become like living planets moving in the orbits of the activities that, indeed, are their lives. But you are no longer as a planet only struggling to realize its creation, but you become like a solar force, that may give life and nurture all about thee, by drawing them into the light, that indeed can bring them forth, and give them higher consciousness, just by exposure to same.

But they must have their evolution—they must have their free will. For these are not principals of violation of free will. These are principles to uplift—these are principles to offer opportunity. For the One Great Spirit is "no respecter of persons," but offers everyone opportunity to come into the light—offers opportunity to come into a higher dimension and realm of understanding. There is also the opportunity now, to choose—to have the ability now to apply this consciousness, first through healing, and then the consciousness shall spread to others, activating their individual talents, bringing them into fuller understanding of applying those talents within thy society to serve others.

Each person who comes to the complete linkage may then gain the ability to pass on that torch and that light to others, which shall, even as the pyramidal structure dictates, geometrically begin to increase, to where eventually all lights upon the planet shall be as lit from the one torch which is God, and dwells within all. Amen.

Is there desire for further information of the specifics of the technology with which you work?

Ron: Yes.

Deva: Crystals are found to amplify thought. These thoughts, then, are found to range along a universal band for, due to the curvatures of the earth plane, there is, indeed, a limited degree of perception of thoughts that may be perceived upon this plane, although the combination, mathematically, of those thoughts, is infinite.

But the range, spectrum and focus of those thoughts, indeed, function within a limited band of frequency. Thus, you have parameters, without violating the law of infinite thought upon this plane, and infinite creation without end.

The device that is currently under construction, may allow individuals full focus to that periphery of thought, and it shall bring their own thoughts of both mind and spirit into total alignment within the proper spectrum and band of expression that is unique to their expression in the earth plane.

For the spiritualization of their personality, they have chosen to dwell along a specific spectrum of that band of thought; and being that this device has the capacity to represent the full-spectrum of creative thought upon this plane, it would draw them naturally into their own alignment of thought. The apparatus is, indeed, a construct of an evolution that the chakras shall undergo. Indeed, it is an ethereal construct of the subtle anatomies of man as he moves into the New Age.

By having the device focused as a physical presence upon the plane, and by working in attunement, it shall eventually draw those whose chakras are exposed to it into the alignment that its physical construct adheres to. The subtle anatomies and the auric properties of the individual would actually begin to take on the dimensions, the peripheries, and the shape of the ethereal patterns that are generated from this particular device.

The device itself is an amplifier that indeed generates the full spectrum of creative thought upon this plane. Then it will become activated by a projection of consciousness from the higher plane—from One whom Deva serves, or seeks to learn further from, One who has observed the activities of the plane since the foundations of the world.

When that consciousness is then projected, the limited spectrum of thought upon this plane becomes aligned with the divine and becomes the fuller expression of the angelic nature, which all of you are, and all of you will become.

Therefore, it is through the alignment of creative thought with divine thought that individuals shall come more fully home, and more fully in alignment. These properties [of alignment] shall then be transferred to the physical body, not only in limited physical healing, for this is but the first test. The device may also seek to align the physical body more fully in the nature of the divine, allowing for perpetual self-regeneration and healing.

But these are only if the individual accepts, these are only if the individual fully works with this energy. There would arise within individuals intuitive methods of meditation—intuitive inspirations to carry out their life's work. This is because the whole physical of the temple that is the living body would then become charged or amplified with the energies from the instrument, aligning them also with the creative thought. With the creative thought then aligned with the divine, they would be fully inspired—wholly transformed by these exposures.

The principles ye work with are still, as though, *magnetic.* The body, indeed, produces and synthesizes many of its own magnetic elements. Constantly, there passes through the physical form the substances known as magnetite. Magnetite, passing through the physical form, when coming into alignment with any mild fields, be they ethereal or magnetic, is one of the principles that helps to align and stabilize the *human aura.*

Magnetite is a substance that helps to align and stabilize the human aura, and would gradually increase in individuals who are exposed to ethereal healing.

This substance would be found to be increased slowly within the physical body upon the cellular levels as individuals come into greater and greater exposures to ethereal healings. Eventually, this substance may even become like a nutrient and be considered normal within the physical diet.

This, then, aligns the individual to where there is actually a process of physiology to be able to enter into, more and more, the states of the divine. Thus, this is why it has been chosen with you, as a healer, to bring forth these things and anchor them well within the physical of the individual, who has first to heal, then to actually anchor the consciousness within the realms and the perimeters of the body physical. For the interjection of mind and body, the individual must go beyond this—they must come to the totality of the knowledge of themselves as the divine.

This is why there is now the moving away from the use of physical supplements in your vibrational healing, except for where intuition shall call for it. The individual shall move more and more fully towards, not healing with light, but, indeed, stimulating the whole individual with light.

I, Deva, must depart now, lest the frequency of self become disruptive to the physical expression speaking [Kevin].
Elohim Adonai

Tom: Back again. How are you doing there?

Ron: Beautiful!

Tom: Quite an impressive fellow.

Ron: What did you experience from your end, Tom?

Tom: Oh, it was quite interesting. The Irish are not without their own forms of meditation, you know, and I just, more or less, stood back and enjoyed the frequency, shall we say. Quite a fascinating energy. A moment please ... may I have a minute to re-orient myself. I believe I am a bit what you call "spacey" for the moment.

Did the discourse help you to pick up a few pieces as things were said?

Ron: Yes, and the feeling of being with Deva was incredible.

Tom: Excellent!

Ron: Perhaps, you, Tom, could tell me a little bit about the types of changes that are happening within me now as a result of exposure to the generator, and what I might expect in the future.

Tom: Fairly easy here. What is taking place at the first level is emotional expungements.

There has also been a rapid evolution in your personal healing practice, and a quickening of your own intellect through the exposure to these crystals, and mind you, it is not only information that comes in from the Friend—it is also information that comes from your own quickened intellect. This is part of the field of creative thought that Deva was speaking of.

Your exposure to the device has heightened your awareness of the outer limits of your planet and its limited thoughts. These then come rushing back to you with their infinite variety and possible combinations. The key thing is not to have you drown in these inspirations. Your own chakras have come nicely into alignment, but they are being held back just a wee bit from total alignment, so that you can still maintain the peripheries of the human personality. When one comes into your office you are still there, and not just as a ball of light floating around the room.

Ron: Which is how I am now starting to feel.

Tom: You can understand why, to have perfection, there must be a slight degree of imperfection. It allows individuals to feel that they can, indeed, obtain to those planes, as well as keep their human personality intact. One of the things that can transpire when working with impersonal energies is not that the individuals themselves must become impersonal—that is a whole different realm and transition of consciousness.

It is that there must still be a fluidity of human empathy and sympathy, thus creating the various noble acts of charity, consciousness and so forth. That is why some of our conversations are just a wee bit sluggish, so as to keep the human factor in them.

Also, blocks of detailed information are being given to you now that would not have come to you through your own direct meditations. They are coming to you through your conversational linkages with the Friend.

For instance, Deva offered the concept of the generator as a fourth and fifth dimensional mandala, and a focus that the higher self can meditate upon constantly. The Giza Pyramid is one such apparatus that is a fourth and fifth dimensional mandala, but your pyramid is to bring the energies directly to the individual. The Giza Pyramid is much more for the masses. Do you see that?

Ron: The Giza Pyramid is more for the masses, whereas the structure I am building can be more specific for an individual, where energy can be directly sent to them?

Tom: Absolutely! The pyramid is an amplifier. Actually, what Deva was attempting to clarify is that the physical design of your pyramid is like the anatomy of the New Age individual. That's why it was critical to have one of the crystals installed in the device that has all seven of its chakras intact.

There are also other changes that you are undergoing. Your own subtle anatomies have been brought into alignment with this mandala. Eventually you will become like a crystal to the point that the energy can then be transferred to other individuals through you. You might notice certain physical changes, such as a greater clarity of blue in the eyes or clearness to the skin tone, and eventually more clarity of thought as you continue to work with these technologies.

The Friend wishes to bring in a completely alternative system of ethereal technology verses just the promotion of electronic and mechanistic types of technologies, in order to offset the growth of man going down the path of worshiping the computer as his new idol.

Do you have a specific inquiry that comes to mind here?

Ron: Yes. Who is the Friend and why did he choose me? What story stands behind our present communication?

Tom: A moment, I will have to check with Deva on this one.

Here is what I may divulge at this time, through myself as an instrument. Some of your history is that this entire activity extends above and beyond just the activity of this plane. It involves several activities where you have passed through what is known as other universes.

Ron: You mean other planes of existence?

Tom: No. Try other universes. Part of what the generator is all about is that there is to be a linkage, possibly, between universes, coming up fairly soon.

Part of that linkage often takes place through the collective consciousness of a single planet. Your planet, because of some rapid evolution that it is undergoing, and because of its constant hovering on the edge of its own man-made holocaust, is graduating into the New Age not only for itself, but there may actually be a direct linkage with another *parallel universe*[3] coming up. Do you understand that?

Ron: I just understand your words …

Tom: It is not that there is a graduation for merely your planet—there are a whole number of planets getting ready to go through a similar transition. There is an entire parallel universe that is also coming into alignment. This is said mostly as an inspiration, rather than being a particular focus that would distract you or scatter your thoughts. It is offered as a wee bit of a higher vision of yourselves, but at the same time the attempt is to keep the work personal.

As to your histories, you were once former occupants of this parallel universe. You have had an entire chronological history of past-lives relative to experiences upon this plane. As this universe comes into alignment, you and other individuals will have a sympathetic resonance with this other universe. Do you see?

Ron: I hear what you're saying. I'll just have to experience it.

Tom: A moment. Your device, along with other devices similar to it across the planet, are being set up, somewhat like needles for treating acupuncture points, to align the planet's meridians with its major chakras. The meridians and the chakras of the planet are being activated by the consciousness of various individuals on this plane.

Ron: On this earth plane?

Tom: Quite right. You are to be somewhat the carriers of information in an attempt to link up enough individuals with the planet's seven chakras. This will allow the seven chakras of the planet to come into alignment with the seven peripheral regions, which are the Pleiades, Orion, Sirius, and … I don't believe Deva wishes to divulge the other four at this time.

When the planet's chakras come into alignment with those of this other parallel universe, this parallel universe will then be able to come into existence. I believe that the Friend was one of the architects of that parallel universe.

Ron: Is this parallel universe non-physical at this time?

Tom: To its own perception it is entirely physical. To your position it is ethereal.

Ron: Could I have a little more information from Deva about who he is and how he works with me in this process?

Tom: Deva is a soul who has taken a unique interest in the affairs of the earth plane. The vibration of Lemuria is what, possibly, originally drew this particular presence to the Earth. He works constructively with the various levels and planes of light in an attempt to rekindle mankind's sense of at-one-ment with the totality of the planet. You, in your own pursuit of natural healing, are, as mentioned, straddling the points of the planet of either extreme ecology or extreme technology. Deva likes that balance and, therefore, has chosen to work with you. Also, Deva was originally one of the citizens of this parallel universe that we speak of, and one of those to first pass through the portal of that universe to become totally activated within this realm and this plane. Do you understand that?

Ron: Well, I heard you, but I'm a long way from understanding what you mean.

Tom: He is carrying a "dual citizenship." His peculiar interest in this plane, and in your work, is that you share a common history with Deva for this particular focus. You are balanced enough and humane enough, so that the work would not totally absorb you into it, or seduce you, but you are enthusiastic enough about it to get the job done. Do you see that then?

Ron: Yes.

Tom: I am sorry. I believe that is all I may communicate at this time. We offer you a vocabulary for communication to other persons, so they can understand these things one drop at a time. Is there more information that you desire here, as I believe we must be departing soon, so that we do not drain the physical instrument?

Ron: No. That's enough. I just want to thank you, Tom.

Tom: Very good. It has been very pleasant speaking with you, and I do hope we have been of aid. Saints be looking after you, and God bless you.

Summary

- The time will come when awareness of spirit will be accepted as a social force, rather than being merely considered a personal belief or superstition.
- By having a fully functioning eighth chakra, we will be able to maintain a direct link with our higher self.
- Planetary consciousness will develop through our alignment with the planetary forces, uniting humanity across the globe.

- The technology of light will help quicken the pulse of consciousness upon this plane, and by quickening it, balance the higher forces, creating a network of light between individuals.

- Alignment of our chakras with the seven planetary energy centers will create a sympathetic resonance, sculpting and cleansing our subtle anatomies of any imbalances.

- Being patient and accepting our own physical healing will eventually lead us to the higher realms of consciousness.

- Eventually, there will be the abandonment of all physical forms of ethereal technologies, for we will become the technology itself.

- The fulfillment of the totality of the self will lead to a merging of the conscious, subconscious and super-conscious.

- Magnetite is a substance that helps to align and stabilize the human aura, and will gradually increase in those exposed to ethereal healing.

1. In human terms, *technology* refers to devices created with scientific knowledge for the purpose of serving humanity. In divine terms, the human form itself appears to be the highest manifestation of spiritual technology, and is based on various organized levels of energy and light.

2. Certain cells, called *pyramidal* cells, located within the cortex of the human brain, appear to function as liquid crystals, having the ability to convert electromagnetic frequencies into subtle electrical currents. These currents, via the nervous system, might conceivably be able to control the entire body. When sensitized to the environment of light, magnetite, when working in conjunction with the pyramidal cells, might actually have the capacity to alter the genetic functions found within the cellular DNA. Controlling the DNA that is located within the stem cells found throughout the body might conceivably allow the physical form to undergo continuous tissue repair and regeneration.

3. Tom is referring to the possibility of the existence of another universe that is about to come into alignment with our own.

Raising Global Awareness

Recently, I came across a quote by cartoonist Bill Watterson, the creator of *"Calvin and Hobbes"* who pointed out that "the surest sign that intelligent life exists elsewhere in the universe is that none of it has tried to contact us." Each joke possesses a grain of truth, and after a minute of laughter, I shifted into reflecting on the bitter reality behind what I had just read.

If we look realistically at the current world situation we will realize that our civilization is precariously poised between self-annihilation and transformation into a new age. Suspended between these two extremes, we find ourselves with the option of either choosing the path of growing understanding and responsibility for our actions, or remaining oblivious to the increasing momentum bringing us down the road of wars, famine, epidemics and natural cataclysms.

It is important to realize that events such as the Indian Ocean tsunami in 2004 which washed away over 250,000 human lives, or hurricane Katrina in 2005 that created 90,000 square miles of destruction, are not signs of an inevitable apocalypse that we are destined to face, but are indicators that we ourselves are creating changes on our planet that have far reaching and devastating results.

In his book, *Divine Wind: The History and Science of Hurricanes*, Kerry Emanuel, one of the world's foremost authorities on hurricanes, describes his research on global warming[1] and its effect on storms that have their origin out at sea. He finds a strong correlation between the global warming of the ocean's surface and an increasing power of hurricanes, reminding us that the ability of nature to sustain our numerous assaults has its limits, and that our time to fully realize this is running out.

The vast majority of scientists agree that there is overwhelming and undeniable evidence that global warming is real and that it is already happening.

Numerous facts unmistakably show that glaciers are melting, plants and animals are being forced from their habitat, and the number of severe storms and other natural cataclysms is increasing.

In the startling documentary *An Inconvenient Truth*[2], former Vice President Al Gore presents a compelling look at the state of global warming, clearly demonstrating that it is the result of our activities, and not just a natural occurrence. In his "traveling global warming show," Gore reveals the stirring truth about planetary warming by exposing the myths and misconceptions that surround it. He calls out to ordinary citizens to address what he calls a "planetary emergency" before it is too late to save the planet from irrevocable changes.

It is hard not to agree with Al Gore's convincing argument that we can no longer afford to view global warming as a political issue—rather, it is one of the biggest moral challenges facing our global civilization.

In the midst of natural disasters, many of us discover that our current systems of social services are often inadequate or ineffective, letting *us* decide either we are ready to take the responsibility into our own hands or simply continue lamenting our fate. We might as well accept that governments themselves are becoming increasingly burdened by economic difficulties, along with social and armed conflicts that are literally leaving them unable to provide the security and support that we would all like to have available to us.

Early in the 20th century the psychic Edgar Cayce claimed that in Earth's ancient past, the misguided civilization of Atlantis unwittingly created cataclysmic changes in the Earth through the misuse of technology, bringing its own destruction. If this is the case, history may not have to repeat itself—we may still have the power to learn from the past, and to create a new future.

1. The observed increase in the average temperature of the Earth's atmosphere and oceans in recent decades. The primary causes of the human-induced component of planetary warming are the increased amounts of carbon dioxide (CO_2) and other greenhouse gases. They are released by the burning of fossil fuels, land clearing, and agriculture, etc. and lead to an increase in the greenhouse effect.

2. A film directed by Davis Guggenheim, featuring Al Gore.

6

Planetary Consciousness

"Our scientific power has outrun our spiritual power. We have guided missiles and misguided men".

~Martin Luther King Jr.

This was the first of a series of three sessions [chapters 6, 7 and 8] that took place over two days late in the fall of 1982 in Marin County, California. Since my last session with Deva about six months earlier, I had felt that I was never alone while treating patients. A flow of thoughts, along with visual images, was continuously sent my way, step by step guiding me in my practice. This guidance was not dominating, but rather like a stream of gentle insights and suggestions on the steps in healing. At any time I felt free to choose my actions, but it became easier and easier to enter a flow of "inaction in action," operating from a place of pure awareness instead of rational thought.

Since I was keenly interested in the pyramids' position throughout history, in this channeling Tom would explain that the pyramids were already known in Lemuria. There they were used for maintaining citizens' spiritual awareness, as well as establishing telepathic connections with other spheres and planes of existence.

In the course of Earth's ancient history, the civilization of Atlantis that came after Lemuria eventually became more focused on technological achievements than on the development of consciousness. This eventually led to catastrophic planetary changes, a step backward in mankind's evolution that caused the legendary sinking of the continent of Atlantis.

During the breakdown of the Atlantean culture, a sect of healers known as the *Menders of Karma* sought to help the citizens maintain their connection with spirit through promoting their link with nature. During this time it was also decided to store the current scientific knowledge in the structure that came to be known as the Great Pyramid.

*　　　*　　　*　　　*

Ron: I have come to hear from Deva and the Friend.

Tom: How are you doing there? Let's get right into it.

I would break down the information from Deva and the Friend into several areas: purposes behind the device; how the device may be used at greater distances; identification of what the device is doing on personal, local, geographical, and planetary levels, and how this all ties in to a more universal principle. Does this sound good?

Ron: Yes.

Tom: I will include a bit more information concerning the construction and the principles of the apparatus, by telling you how it was used in past lives in the areas of Egypt. I will also include a part of what the apparatus stimulates, and tie it all in with some of your past-life connections. Is this appropriate for you then?

Ron: Yes.

Tom: Very good. This device was utilized and built upon cultural exchanges in Lemuria during the Atlantean and Lemurian times. Lemuria was the first evolved civilization by the spiritual presence you now call mankind, and was the first Garden of Eden. All individuals of that particular time period existed at one level of consciousness, and everyone was intermingled telepathically. There was literally only one mind on the plane, and everyone shared equally in what was known as the planetary consciousness. This was accomplished through various purifying rituals, and also by philosophically linking oneself with nature, similar to some of the Taoist and Zen Buddhist paths of today. This was part of the practice of the Lemurians, and it came to them naturally.

In order to evolve the next step of planetary consciousness, it was necessary to create an entirely new system of sociological forces, thus giving birth to the Atlantean continent, and its creation as a separate and individual society.

Soon, Atlantis began developing technologies at a rapid rate, and the philosophy that was advanced in Atlantis became slightly different from the philosophy of Lemuria. The Lemurians primarily derived all of their consciousness from natural sources and from organic technologies. However, the Atlanteans began to evolve differently, and believed that technology preceded consciousness, rather than consciousness preceded technology. This was a radical difference between the two philosophies of the continents. Atlantis was growing at a rapid rate from new technologies that were evolving, and consequently their philosophy became the dominant one.

This was a slight step downward in the planet's growth. Therefore, in order to preserve the best elements of both Lemuria and Atlantis, there occurred the evolution of the Egyptian and Indian schools of thought. It was during the co-existence of Lemuria and Atlantis that the construction of devices similar to yours first came into usage. Therefore, the pyramids and the crystals were a merger of both Lemurian and Atlantean technologies, plus utilizing a healthy exchange with dwellers from other planets.

These dwellers on other planets came from the influences of Orion, the Pleiades and Sirius.

The Atlanteans primarily opened up diplomatically, socially, and politically, to beings from other spheres as well. The technologies that you are currently developing were being utilized at that time to enhance communication with the beings from those spheres.

The key element here is the next evolution that you are about to step into, which is a reactivation of your knowledge of individuals from other planes and other spheres of existence. Above all else, this will involve the creation of an esoteric society of individuals who will be able to work with these principles, whatever their beliefs, philosophies or circumstances might be.

You had many of your past-lives during incarnations in Lemuria, as well as in Atlantis. There, you were a member of the priesthood who knew that Lemuria could not survive the cultural shock that it was experiencing by importing Atlantean philosophies. You were aware that Lemuria was about to undergo its final submerging.

Ron: Physical submerging, or cultural?

Tom: Both, actually.

You were a member of the Lemurian priesthood who were attempting to bring as much of the surviving Lemurian sciences and culture to Atlantis as possible. This came about with the cooperation of the devic realms, which are the realms that you consider to be nature spirits. You realized that in order for the society to remain healed in consciousness, it was critical that it stay interwoven with beings from the spiritual dimensions, and with the various levels of its own spiritual and esoteric histories.

Ron: Can you tell me what my role was at that time in relation to what I am doing now?

Tom: You were responsible for creating architecture and techniques of healing to preserve a society, or priesthood, where individuals could continue to practice various free-will principles.

Whereas, before, you had an entire population to draw-upon in Lemuria, now there were merely the scattered remnants of the Lemurians amongst the Atlantean population. Your technology, at that time, was designed to enhance soul memories and to bring individuals back into alignment with spirit.

Your karma and past experiences upon this plane are the key elements as to how the individual shapes their life-purpose, and above all else, how they shape their own spiritual, mental and physical wellbeing and healing. When all of those properties merge together, they become inspiration as to how the individual will shape the rest of their life-purpose for the duration of their physical plane incarnation.

You became a member of an order, or sect, known as the "Menders of Karma."

Ron: That is how it feels now.

Tom: Most definitely. After a period of time, the Atlantean's knowledge of crystals was eventually turned aside from spiritual pursuits, and the crystals were eventually used for more mundane applications, such as the generation of electrical power.

Technology became a process of gathering knowledge to be applied for the society as a whole. The society began indulging in what I would call "the pleasure principle." Rather than cooperating with technology, their desire was to enslave it and have it become their servant. Thus, the sense that the life force flows through everything, including the planet and crystals as living beings, was lost.

You wished to keep alive the idea of integrating the person with the whole of everything, but as the principles and philosophies that were primarily Lemurian began to fade from the Atlantean society, your sector of the priesthood became known as "elitists."

Ron: You mean we were indeed elitists?

Tom: No. It gave the *illusion* that you were elitists. To continue to preserve the technologies, it became necessary that you only practice with those souls who had clearer memories of the Lemurian society. Eventually, the established priesthood along with the merchants, the working class, and those with scientific inclination governed your influence in the society. This fourfold governing of society continued to deteriorate, and your priest class was eventually reduced to no more than a mystery school status. The forces truly governing the Atlantean society became those of the scientific bent and those of the merchants, both of which eventually became the dominant economic force—the laboring class eventually became enslaved by the merchants.

It was at this particular point of the continuing social decay of Atlantis, that the priesthood came up with a plan for preparing various means for storing the remaining knowledge of the spiritual dimensions in the structure known as the Great Pyramid. There was a twofold form of storing the knowledge. The Pyramid was to contain all of the necessary information for those who could decipher its codes of geometrical and mathematical principles of energy. There was also to be a separate Hall of Records, where information would be stored physically in hieroglyphic form, on tablets made of various elements, such as emerald and quartz. It is still decipherable by the linguistic standards of the day. The Atlantean and Lemurian languages are stored primarily in Hindi, Chinese, Egyptian, *Nubian*, and a few other languages, and are still traceable.

Devices such as yours were used for a threefold purpose: first, the exposure to its energies would reintegrate the person with the planetary consciousness; second, it was used for tapping the information stored in the pyramids and in the Hall of Records; third, it aligned the person with the information that came from other spheres and other planes of existence— primarily from the Pleiades, Orion, and Sirius.

Does this past-life review help to clarify potential applications for the device and its purposes?

Ron: Yes, the work is basically being done on an energetic level. Correct?

Tom: Yes. The reason for focusing on this level of information is to keep your perspective, so as not to create yet another religion. This will allow you to appreciate the device as an applicable technology, and as an educational experience. These types of devices will eventually come to be used commonly in society, if not now, then at such a time when a broader acceptance of them is appropriate for the planet.

Ron: Will the people who are ready for the device get the benefit of it now?

Tom: Quite right. And perhaps they would be the carriers of it to the next generation, if necessary. It has always been this way. If you want to know the truth, Nikola Tesla[1] created such a device about a hundred years ago— however, the planet was not quite ready for it.

We will go ahead and take our leave now. It is has been very pleasant speaking with you. Saints be looking after you. God bless you.

Summary

- In the early days of our ancient past, there was literally one mind on the plane, and everyone shared in what was known as the planetary consciousness.

- Our past experiences upon this plane are key elements in shaping our current life purpose, along with our spiritual, mental and physical wellbeing.

- Pyramidal devices have a three-fold purpose: integrating a person with the planetary consciousness, accessing information, and aligning an individual with other spheres and planes of existence.

1. Nikola Tesla (1856–1943) was a Serbian inventor and physicist respected for his research into electricity and magnetism. After he first demonstrated wireless communication in 1893, he gained the reputation as America's greatest electrical engineer, and became known as the inventor of the radio. In his later years, Tesla was regarded as a mad scientist for making fantastic claims about possible scientific developments regarding energy and health.

The Story Behind the Pyramid

As the construction of the pyramidal device began to take shape, I found myself more and more intrigued by the possibilities that geometrical forms potentially offered.

I wondered if certain geometrical structures might function as three-dimensional mandalas, and if different shapes resonate with universal energy fields, much like a piano string produces a sound in resonance with the same note played on another instrument.

The pyramidal device itself would be a tubular framework housing a number of large crystals, and big enough for several people to meditate in. Fascinated by the experience of two-way communication with spirit guides and by the possibility of exploring the unknown, I never questioned the opportunity to delve into this project.

The work on the pyramid continued over a period of three to four years. Although the engineering and glass companies both did their job in due time, I still needed to gather my resources and to arrange the meetings with Kevin for further instructions from the spirit guides, all of which was time consuming. I had also been able to locate one of the last large single crystals to come out of Arkansas, the place in the United States that provided most of the quartz for the entire country.

Eventually a connection was made with Ida Oberstein, a small town in Germany that was the only location where I could find a high quality crystal ball twelve inches in diameter. I flew there, procured several large crystals, and returned home with my precious cargo that traveled in its own airline seat right next to me.

One day, during the construction of the pyramid, when I was visiting the small engineering company that was building it, the workers had an interesting story to tell me. They had watched their cat, who lived in the shop where the construction was taking place, begin to cross the room by taking a shortcut right through the center of the newly assembled tubular framework of the pyramid. Intriguingly, the animal had stopped mid-step, just as it had begun to enter the pyramid itself. It looked around, as if sensing the presence of someone or some energy field, apparently completely taken aback by what it was feeling. Then, it gently drew its paw out of the pyramid, walked backwards two steps, and proceeded to cross the room by walking around the outside of the pyramid, completely circumventing the entire structure. The workers said that they had owned the cat for many years, and yet had never seen such unusual behavior in its whole life. They also added that, during the next several weeks of completing the construction, the cat never even went near the pyramid again, and would cross from one side of the room to the other by walking against one of the walls of the warehouse.

This led me to entertain the possibility that the pyramidal form itself, even as a tubular framework that was under construction, could already possess qualities that created some type of energy field in its immediate environment.

7

The University of Illumination

"All truths are easy to understand once they are discovered;
the point is to discover them".

~Galileo Galilei

This meeting took place on the morning following my last session, and was the second channeling in a series of three. The more I communicated with Deva and the Friend the more ecstatic I felt during these meetings with spirit. Listening to my guides, I experienced being in the presence of pure consciousness and love.

In this session I was taught that we come to the earth plane not only for making a temporary journey through matter, but also for reawakening to the knowledge that we are beings of energy and light. As this transformation takes place, it will not necessarily lead to the development of various psychic faculties, but to a conscious awareness of the environment of light, which may be aided by technologies like the pyramidal device. With this new, yet ancient, technology, the physical body will become the *divine conductor,* resulting in physical and spiritual well-being, along with an expansion of consciousness.

*　　　　*　　　　*　　　　*

Ron: I have come hoping to hear from Deva and the Friend.

Tom McPherson here. How're you doing there?

Ron: I'm doing well. Tom, what has your experience been with Deva and the Friend since beginning these sessions?

Tom: Quite frankly, it has been a recapping back to my old days in Atlantis, and working off some of the karmic experiences from that particular time period. In fact, you and I have known each other in those lifetimes where I was working with crystalline structures and various forms of surgery. In that lifetime I described myself as an Atlantean surgeon, but it had nothing to do with the whittling of the flesh, so much as it had to do with the cleansing of the auric faculties.

You see, the entity called Tom McPherson, or the entity that is speaking right now, is really quite unique in his own right. He can be funny or fallible, all of which goes into the human dimension. He also has a portion of the identity from an Atlantean lifetime called Alurus. That entity called Alurus, and the entity called Tom McPherson, are able to merge and blend together, forming a whole new identity. Mind you, it is the evolution of Tom McPherson. Actually, Tom McPherson is the entity whose vocabulary and Earth perspective is being used now. A whole new entity would come about from the merger of Tom McPherson and the entity Alurus, moving closer to the soul frequency experienced in both of those lifetimes. That is what your crystal device does. It integrates all aspects of a person's karmic pattern to where they become a whole new person.

Is there more inquiry here, then?

Ron: What was your experience when Deva said he wanted to talk to you directly? That was where he took you to levels of pure energy?

Tom: Oh, absolutely. That was the beginning of the point of merging towards the spiritual. That is the point of pure energy, where a person can get in touch with the sum total of the whole of their past lives. It is almost one of the points where information will be disseminated through this crystal structure. It is the point at which the soul begins to merge with all the aspects of its different identities and becomes a purely objective experience on the earth plane. It is suspended somewhere between the universal consciousness and the planetary consciousness.

Perhaps one or two more inquiries, and then I believe your friendly neighborhood helpers can come in.

Ron: I would like a clarification of the different levels, such as the physical, etheric, etc. Which of them are separate vehicles of consciousness and on what level does Deva come through? My understanding is that the physical and etheric are one level; the next level is the emotional, mental, and astral; then causal, and finally spiritual.

Tom: The level Deva works upon is that of the spiritual and causal, mostly dwelling on the causal. The causal plane allows for the shaping and evolvement of individuals from the spiritual level. The astral, mental, and emotional is where a person begins a physical incarnation into the earth plane. By not possessing a physical form, beings such as Deva remain in the spiritual and causal dimensions.

I believe Deva would like to come through and address a series of issues concerning this work, if you like.

Deva: Here then, the presence of Deva. I, then, who have been identified as Deva, would come forth to speak with you according to those things that you would seek to manifest in the earth plane in these days. Many are the eons past before these things were to come forth and bring forth new wisdom—to seek to reintegrate the planetary methodologies as a whole; to reactivate the ancient principles, wherein the consciousness of man-and woman-kind may flow ever upward and become at one again with the planetary levels.

For those things that you would seek to bring forth in a fullness and an understanding are wisdoms in their own right to pursue. To begin to understand these things, the transformation is always within the individual. For that which you begin to assist is to restore to the planet an environment of light.

Even as there has been the development of the philosophies that man-and womankind must make a sojourn, as though, into nature itself, in order to come to a fulfillment, a greater fulfillment, and knowledge of themselves as beings of nature and at one with that force called nature. In turn, there must also be the acknowledgement of the environment of light upon the physical plane, for it is the environment of light that men and women truly inhabit, and it is this that you seek to restore.

The gift of this particular venture is the sensitization of individuals again to that environment of light, so that it may then become an active principle in their daily affairs. This sensitization is not, however, a seeking or heightening of the psychic faculties, but rather a sensory increase to the environment of light, and the impact that it has upon persons.

For even as you become knowledgeable about the afflictions that are brought upon humankind as a whole from the alterations in the environment, and the polluting of that self-same environment that afflicts you physically, so in turn must you become more knowledgeable of the benevolence of the environment of light which you have always inhabited—as the mental, spiritual and physical being.

The whole of thy wellbeing is based on being bathed in the environment of light. The apparatus that you have brought forth has its linkages to the very core and foundation of this world. That planetary force is then purified by passing through the crystalline structures contained within the device, and is then linked with the seven critical points upon the planet. That force shall then stream outward into the whole and the heritage of the planet and into the planetary consciousness itself, and shall then find linkage with the higher dimensions, which are still contributing origins to portions of thy physical being—those who travel beyond this sphere and contribute to the environment of light upon the plane.

Then individuals will become fully sensitized and fully re-centered upon their original course of evolution as physical, mental and spiritual beings.

For so long has the planet dwelled in darkness, for so long have there only been the few who have known these things, that the planet has lost many of the courses of its original inspiration, and you have come to be dependent only upon the five physical senses. So thus the organizations of thy bodies of sciences, which call themselves but the "physical sciences," and you have come to shape your environment and your learning only by these.

You have now come to restore a *science of light*—a technology of light, from which you have created a center-point of learning, a center-point of experience to re-align with that environment of light. You are seeking to create a point of a *university of light*—a *university of illumination*, from whence individuals shall come forth and become clearer channels, by removing from them any blockages. In the physical dimension these would be felt as rejuvenation as you would term physical wellbeing. But this is only so that the body may become the divine conductor. For the divine conductor of the physical form is to be likened to fine metals through which pass electrical forces. And those electrical forces, and the metals in their purity, merge and become various technologies that drive great engines that move thy society.

So in turn must the physical form be made the clear conductor. The by-products of these shall be healing, as the greater patterns and illuminations of light come forth, where each individual becomes sensitive to the whole of the body of the planet, and realize themselves to be citizens of that. For they shall overcome limitations in consciousness, limitations in their social framework, and realize that they are *citizens of a planetary nature*, and they shall recognize no boundaries, and recognize no functions, and no duties, and no oath, except unto the higher forces.

Ye would call this "overcoming limited social and psychological frameworks of reference." Thus, the mental also becomes healed and senses wellbeing.

As to the spiritual, here an individual who is exposed to the device would experience a continuous and knowledgeable frequency of light, as to be totally inspired, as with no separation from that light, but to become totally clarified and totally purposeful in it.

These would be the alterations that you would see in the personality: formerly, where there was only the self, there becomes altruism. Formerly, were there was only the intellectual, there becomes the divine mental. Formerly, where there may have only been the agnostic, there becomes the total awareness of the spiritual.

But these changes are to be gradual within the self, so as not to interfere with the patterns of one's life, for it is when the individual accepts these as an active and pragmatic sector of the self that they become fully realized. You will therefore establish the principals of "pragmatic spirituality," integrated in ways such that they become the most helpful and beneficial.

You will find first here in the construction of the crystalline device, that you work with the model of the whole human dimension. You will first find the drawing-up of the energy from the Earth through the seven levels of existence, and then the linking in special uniqueness of each individual to the planetary whole.

Then, the three crystalline structures dwelling above [three crystal balls within the *capstone* of the pyramid] will become representative of the linkages with the true self, and indeed, with the dimensions of the higher self. They have representation with three linkages of import upon the planet, and with three points of experience from within the whole of a federation of living beings, indeed, even those who were observed by Ezekiel[1].

So even as you draw forth sustenance from the Earth, and from the core of the Earth, and these pass through seven spiritual seats of consciousness in the physical form, you have within the model of the crystalline structure the model of the human condition. And being that it is pure and crystalline in its nature, then others may align to it, with it serving as the pattern.

For here you will have constructed a geometrical and fourth-and fifth-dimensional model of that which can be considered the *Christ consciousness* for the individual. But this, however, is but the pattern, and what ye are working with are the activities of three-dimensional and four-dimensional mandalas.

In the Eastern systems of thought, the mandalas have been the activators of the spiritual seats of consciousness within the physical form. Here, with the apparatus, you have moved these into the third and fourth dimensions—then you have linked them to the whole of the planet, where they become the conductors, and the anchorers of fields of energy, so that the individual may then become the student.

By entering within its walls [of the pyramid], or being within the perimeter of its energy fields, there is then the clear channel for first promoting physical wellbeing. This allows the physical form to align all of its own subtle anatomies, aiding and promoting the elements of its own physical wellbeing. This allows the body to then become the clear conductor, to then receive the information that would come forth from the three higher spherical forms within the apparatus, to reintegrate with the history of the planet as a whole.

But that unit which remains to be set [the large quartz sphere] allows the individual an even greater gift—the gift of fellowship, to externalize the self unto the waiting soul groups, the center-point of creating stronger bonds and linkages within the soul groups, wherein the individuals may begin to actualize their own life pattern within their own higher spiritual dimensions. *Self-actualizing* is the greatest gift of all, for you grant them freedom within the midst of the ocean of cosmic knowledge and cosmic choice. When they become the clearer conductors, and the light becomes self-actualizing from the higher self, rather than from the baser self, then in turn the light becomes the greater gift. They become actualized in their own spiritual dimensions, each contributing to the planet to the ability of their highest achievement—even if they know not fully the things that they aspire unto, but eventually becoming fully knowledgeable of same.

Are these things to your assimilation at this time?

Ron: Yes.

Deva: Is there desire for point of any clarification of that which has been wrought?

Ron: At this time, no.

Deva: Further then: you will begin to work with and reactivate the ancient technologies. The ancient technologies of being are to bring forth the critical focal points of the ancient wisdom as from Atlantis, Lemuria and *Atalon*, then also the energies collectively of the dimensions of the Pleiades, Orion, Sirius and the others contained therein, in these dimensions, and in and of their ancient wisdoms.

You shall seek to bring forth individuals into the whole of their own exposures—the whole of their own patterns. This is what is desired to be given at this time.

Tom: Back again. How are you doing there?

Ron: Fine, Tom. [Tom and I were there together in the presence of Love. What more could I say?]

Tom: Very good. If I could ground-out a bit as to what Deva was implicating, then I believe that Deva would like to come back and give a bit of a bibliography, or a listing of spots that your device is designed to activate.

Ron: Sounds good to me.

Tom: First of all, did you understand what Deva was saying? He was attempting to communicate that you are establishing what he called a *university of illumination*. In other words, each individual who would come into exposure with this device is, in his or her own right, a repository of information upon the planet. Actually, a good teacher is little more than a repository of linear information, but is then quite clever in the way that they arrange the information when presenting it to others in order to inspire them.

What transpires, then, is that this particular device allows for the loosening up of an individual to become a clear channel for information from some of the celestial points mentioned: the Pleiades etc., but in alignment with their own past history upon this planet, so that it has perspective, and is relevant as well, to this planet. An example would be an architect who might be inspired to build things more along ethereal principles, aligning houses with *ley-lines*, and taking advantage of solar dimensions and things to that effect [solar homes for example].

In any case, it takes individuals to their next level of evolution. The device allows an individual to see what is going on. It is quite alchemical in a way, because it is transformational. If a person desires the higher dimensions, or higher gift, the device would take them into the next level of their personal transformation and align them with their purpose.

Primarily, what Deva is saying is that, indeed, this device aligns body, mind and spirit with the purpose that already exists within the perimeters of the individual. That is what he meant by a university of illumination.

Now, then, would you like Deva to pop back in and give you a bit of a bibliography of some of these areas to look for?

Ron: Absolutely!

Deva: Here, then, we have found the *points of leading and learning*, to be drawn upon by your device and its placement and alignment with the Earth's *fluidiums* and of those things which you have termed the "ley-lines." Here, we find aspects and points of learning, some of which have been revealed through other sources, but through this instrument at this time. We would find the Great Pyramid of the Sun[2] in that city which you know as Mexico. We also find a place of learning known as Chichen Itza. We also find Tiahuanaco. We also find the great place of Giza. We also find Luxor. We also find the dimensions of Stonehenge. We also find The Great Serpent Mound by Five Bodies of Water.

We find these to be as the places of leading and learning desired to be given as a map of consciousness at this time. You will find that the activities of the individuals who are attracted to the device have been many at these points. We also find points of learning in Tibet and India, and in pyramidal forms in China. These shall be isolated [discovered] in later days.

Each of these points of learning is where the individuals shall first come into alignment with the seven great seats of consciousness upon the planet, then the individual knowledges by which they may more carefully weave the tapestry of their personalities from past lives. The function of healing in the physical form is to allow the physical form to become the clearer conductor. The individuals would also be able to have an attunement to alignment with the planetary consciousness.

Therefore, many of the dimensions of your work are to create channels: channels for the divine, and channels to become aligned with the natural laws and forces of the universe.

Here you will find that those things known as the devic realms are the natural forces as they align with the laws governing this plane. And then when you find the archangels and the angels, you will find these to be synonymous with the laws that govern the universe, in the greater whole itself.

Thus these things are given personage, thus these things are given voice, through these various instruments that would then serve those higher forces, so that they will, as in scripture, become no longer under the law, but *become* the law—taking them to the levels of the causal plane, and becoming again the causal force upon the planet, rather than being the reactor to same.

The device will activate the individual, rather than allowing the individual to react to each of those individual experiences and information that come to them, and allow them to become the causal force, taking them to the next levels of their transformation.

Is there desire for clarification of these principles?

Ron: At this time, no. [I answered briefly because, in having this time with Deva, I was feeling a growing sense of awe that made it hard to say anything at all.]

Tom: Back again. How are we doing there?

Ron: Fine, Tom.

Tom: Very good. Any further inquiries here on what Deva has given?

Ron: I can't think of any questions now. Well, there is one question regarding the broadcast sphere. Can you define the part that this crystal sphere plays?

Tom: Yes. The broadcast crystal, primarily, is the focal point. Deva was reiterating to you that you have the central crystalline structure with its seven seats of consciousness, which serves to draw up energy from the earth plane. In the same way, biological life was drawn up from the earth plane from inanimate mineral to the plant, then to the animal, and then to the human dimensions. The broadcast crystal, in ethereal principal, does the same thing.

The reason that you have taken on the human dimension in your physical form is no accident of evolution. It is actually the pre-planning of a physical structure that would be shaped around matrixes of energy that come from the seven levels of consciousness. These have been referred to as the various planes. In other words, the human condition is a microcosm of the energy fields that govern this plane. The crystal, with its seven seats of consciousness, represents that.

Your three higher crystals, symbolically, have several purposes. There are three independent levels of information coming in from what are known as archangels, as well as information coming in from three sectors of space that those archangels dwell in. The three crystals represent aspects of what is known as the Father, Son and Holy Spirit.[3]

Ron: Could you clarify Father, Son and Holy Spirit?

Tom: The Father is basically the universal force that is in everything—if you wish to break it down into its physical representation. The Son represents the soul force of an individual. The Holy Spirit represents the revelatory factor.

Ron: I have a new topic. I am not consciously psychic. Can you tell me a little bit about what is happening with my own evolution in consciousness?

Tom: You say you are not consciously psychic. However, would you not say that you are intuitive in some of your healing works?

Ron: Sure.

Tom: Would you not say that you are also occasionally conscious of events before they transpire?

Ron: Sometimes.

Tom: I would say that you are psychic in the sense that you have aligned yourself with the natural flow of things. What you call being consciously psychic is where a person might attempt to manipulate psychic faculties, including one's personal needs in the daily mundane affairs of life. Actually, that can get quite boring and become quite disjointed. If only a person would just attempt to align himself or herself with the higher forces ... I would say that you are more clairvoyant, which means to see clearly, in the tradition of a fellow by the name of Emmanuel Swedenborg[4]. You are more of a visionary individual.

Ron: Tom, in the course of this process, am I going to start seeing auras and colors, and "reading minds" and things like that, or is it going to be different?

Tom: I think that it is only when it is appropriate that these would come to you. For instance, Jesus divined minds when it was appropriate. Above all else, I believe that you are more into the faculties of divining the heart. You are more of an *empath*.

I believe one more inquiry and then I will take my leave, so that we can recharge the instrument. I believe the Friend wishes to dominate the next series of discourses.

Ron: I have no further questions at this time Tom. You can go ahead and give Kevin a rest now, if you like.

Tom: Very good. It's been very pleasant speaking with you.

Summary

- The sensitization to the environment of light is not a heightening of the psychic faculties, but rather a growing awareness of the benevolence of the environment in which we have always inhabited.

- We are to restore a science of light and to create a university of illumination—a center point of learning and experience to re-align with the environment of light.

- As we become clearer conductors of luminosity, we will overcome limitations in consciousness, realizing that we are citizens of a planetary nature.

- The crystalline device serves as a model of the whole human dimension, aligning our subtle anatomies with its crystalline pattern.

- The function of healing in the physical form is to allow the physical form to become the clearer conductor.

1. In the bible story, Ezekiel "saw the wheel," when his spiritual sight opened up and he had a vision of many levels of heavenly hosts.

2. The Pyramid of the Sun was located 25 miles northeast of what is now Mexico City, known before as Teotihuacán, meaning *City of the Gods*. It was probably the largest human settlement in all of the Americas, and the sixth largest city in the world, with as many as 200,000 residents around the sixth century C.E. (It had virtually been abandoned by 900 C.E.). The city was dominated by the Pyramid of the Sun, which stood over 200 feet high and was over 700 feet long, being the third largest pyramid in the world.

3.   Here, the *Father* is the Universal Light, we, as spirit in matter, are the *Sons*, and the *Holy Spirit* is the invisible divine power that supports all of creation through vibration. Knowledge of the Father is available only through experience and not as a concept or belief.

4.   Born in 1688, Swedenborg was a Swedish scientist, inventor and mystic, who later in life began having spiritual visions and talking with angels. He claimed that biblical characters such as Jesus and Moses appeared to him and interpreted the scriptures. Similar transformations have occurred for other famous individuals, such as Immanuel Kant, William Blake, Sir Arthur Conan Doyle and even Carl Jung.

Journey to Chichen Itza

My work on the pyramidal device immensely increased my interest in the mysterious history of pyramids and the civilizations that had erected them thousands of years ago. Following my quest, I decided to take a short leave and go visit one of the sacred Mayan sites in Central America.

Accompanied by my son, Dee, and stepdaughter Lisa, I set course for Cozumel, an island off the east coast of Mexico. Besides offering great scuba diving and snorkeling, Cozumel is only a short flight from Chichen Itza, an ancient Mayan city that is said to possess some of the most fascinating and well-preserved ruins in Mexico.

There, at the center of the Chichen Itza site, stands a huge stone pyramid rising nearly eighty feet into the air. It is known as the Pyramid of Kukulcán, built by the ancient Mayan Toltec, a civilization that flourished in the Yucatan around 800 to 1200 C.E. Strangely, the entire city was abruptly abandoned, and although there are many theories about this sudden exodus, none have yet been successfully substantiated.

After scuba diving for a couple of days in Cozumel, the kids and I headed off for Chichen Itza. Having unloaded from the bus that brought us from the local airport to the actual site, the kids immediately set off to explore in one direction and I went in another.

I was obviously not prepared for what happened next. Suddenly, an intense feeling of deep sorrow overtook me as I entered the site and began walking straight towards the colossal pyramidal structure mounting in the midst of all the other ruins. Unable to explain the cause of this overwhelming sadness, I slowly approached the huge pyramid's base and began climbing up its stony steps, occasionally turning back to look out over the jungle-covered landscape.

As I climbed higher and higher, I observed the entire sight, surrounded by thick green foliage, where only the tops of the tallest trees were visible from the vantage point of the pyramid's height. I eventually reached the summit and, gazing around, started wondering if this had once been a place of sacrifice. Could it be that I had lost someone dear to me on this very spot many centuries ago? I continued to speculate on my thoughts for quite a while, but eventually gave up trying to reason it out.

Gradually, my mind became quiet, and I simply let myself feel the powerful presence of the pyramid's long and tumultuous past. Strangely, sitting on the top of these ancient ruins, I felt remarkably at home. It was as if all pyramids everywhere on this planet were telling the same universal truth, relaying the same cosmic message to mankind. Perhaps they themselves held a secret code to be broadcast to the very stars that I had gazed upon for so many nights.

At that point I had to be patient. The answers to these and other questions would turn up almost fifteen years later, during sessions with Kevin, but until then I would be left to wonder.

8

Countenance of Fellowship

"My religion consists of a humble admiration of the illimitable superior spirit who reveals himself in the slight details we are able to perceive with our frail and feeble mind".

~Albert Einstein

This meeting with Kevin occurred in the afternoon following my morning session held the same day, and was the last in the series of three. During this channeling I felt that I was finally reconnected with my true spiritual family, whom I had longed to be with for many years.

In this session I was introduced to the concept of the *countenance of fellowship*, and learned that Deva was the equivalent of a *tulku*. I also discovered that as ethereal technologies become more common across the planet, celestial light and music[1] will be among the first things that we might experience as a result of coming into alignment with the higher universal forces.

In the healing process of the Earth itself, there will be the reactivation of the ley-lines, leading to relocation of world populations, gradually shifting them towards focal points of energy on the Earth's surface. The relocation of the ley-lines will also create an environment of light on the planet.

*   *   *   *

Ron: I have come to hear further discourse from Deva.

Tom: Back again. How're you doing there?

Ron: I'm doing fine, Tom.

Tom: First of all, any inquiries come to mind before we launch into the whole affair here?

Ron: I am finding myself caring less and less about any particular information, and mostly just longing to hear from Deva and the Friend. I have been realizing that I am even getting attached to them in a personal way.

Tom: It is a countenance of fellowship. What constitutes your strong attraction to Deva and the Friend on personal levels is that, as individuals grow closer to becoming citizens of the environment of light, they sometimes become "more peculiar by social standards," as spirit wishes to put it. Do you understand that?

Ron: Of course.

Tom: The desire to have fellowship with beings that are less corporeal and are more of the spiritual dimensions becomes increasingly attractive to the individual. Therefore, as you continue to develop yourself in this environment of light, the personal attachment becomes a desire for association with others who have an equivalent level of understanding of, shall we say, an equivalent level of appreciation for that same desire for the Light. That is why it is a personal issue with you—it becomes a desire to associate with individuals who are on that level of illumination.

Your own connection with the Friend will develop along these lines, not only in relationship to this particular project, but also in possibly being able to give insight to other individuals. Again, this is a University of Illumination—each person being "a word in the Book of Life."

Perhaps one more inquiry, and then I believe Deva may align, and then the Friend.

Ron: Deva is here for those of us who got caught in the evolutionary cycle of the beings on this planet?

Tom: Absolutely.

Ron: Deva will stay here until this evolution is complete, and we are able to leave the planet with full consciousness?

Tom: Quite right. Deva is the equivalent of what is known as a *tulku* in the Eastern [Tibetan Buddhist] systems of thought. A tulku is one who has taken certain oaths or vows of staying on the plane until certain manifestations are made in the soul group. Deva remains in the devic realms. This is why there have been hints that Deva works on the level of the planetary forces, and has linkages to the higher universal forces.

Ron: But why do I feel such a particular connection to Deva?

Tom: Because Deva is so integrated with your own particular higher self. We have said that this work goes back many, many eons. Deva also has a similar vibrational frequency with your own spiritual teacher on the earth plane. Another reason for the closeness that you have with Deva is that he is one of those that were created within your own soul group when souls were originally initiated. All of you were created in the same sectors of time and space, simultaneously.

Would you like Deva to come through now and give a bit of a discourse?

Ron: Please.

Deva: Again in the light, that each individual would seek to bring; that each individual would seek to bring and merge, and to have understanding of, once again, the re-entry and re-initiation into the environment of light— and that is that no individual may truly go forth until the whole is transformed.

In bringing forth the return again of the environment of light to the physical plane, there shall be activities where there shall be the opening of many of the portals of *celestial sound and light*. The celestial music, of course, has always existed, promoting the hearing and the perceiving by the individual of the natural laws that govern the universe, and your own "at-one-ment" with it. The celestial light is that which brings illumination that the individual is, in truth, aware of only a particle of all the energies and the dynamics that surround you.

In the building of the third and fourth dimensional mandala, the individuals will be introduced to, and become aware of, celestial light and celestial music. These also shape the environment of the individual, but with heightened degrees of consciousness, as the individual would come into a greater and fuller awareness of these things. The celestial light and celestial music may then become more fully tangible, and illumine the individuals into fuller and greater capacities.

These will also become measurable in their results—that detectable invisible environment about you, which your physical sciences measure as electromagnetic frequencies, which will be found to both radiate, and to irradiate [broadcast in a beam] from the device. These fields will be detectable from no single source within the object, but only at times upon the completion of assemblage.

These frequencies are to be for the upliftment and the stimulus of the physical body. Their range will be those frequencies measurable between eleven cycles and sixty cycles per second. These will be detectable upon all the metallic surfaces of the device, as well as radiating from the central crystal that is to be used for the purpose of broadcast.

These energies will bathe the physical body, raising the attunement of the cellular structures more in line with the divine. These will stimulate greater levels of conscious activity, increasing and strengthening the mental bodies of those who choose to be exposed to the device's fields. You would find that the central purpose of the device is to align the person with the highest sense of duty that they may desire, and need to obtain, on this plane.

There are those who would choose knowledge of the spiritual dimensions, and the paths of theology and religiosity, to whom the spiritual appeals—those who would choose to learn knowledgeably about the forces and the masters who created this plane, even as they lived here and from those lives. Then, there are those who desire to be stimulated in the intellect, to be quickened in it, to heighten the intelligence quotient in their particular field of endeavor and skill, and thus to contribute to a growing community as a whole. Also, we find persons who perhaps seek to derive only knowledge from those who traverse time and space itself.

Thus has been created both the personal and the impersonal. The impersonal is in the device itself, and in its application; the personal is that you, as individuals, give and bring forth the personal—the personal revelation. Each of you would then be able to come forth with the capacities and the individual skills stimulated within yourselves to complete you life work. This will bring you to your fulfillment, as individuals, but it is your relationship with the whole of the universal that brings you to fulfillment within the divine.

Adonai

Tom: Back again. Celestial light and celestial music are some of the first things that individuals should begin to experience when coming into alignment with these universal forces.

There is also a peculiar statement that "there are those who live by wells, and there are those who build wells." To a certain degree, you are a builder of a well, in opening up this portal of consciousness.

I believe the Friend would like to speak through.

Ron: Thank you.

The Friend:

Ingro Sototh Esthnoth
Ramatoth Amon
Ranai Oto Adonai

I, who have been called the Friend, would come again to speak to those who would bring into their midst a portal for consciousness, so as to seek to uplift the many.

First, there was the construction of the device, so as to preserve the integrity of the flows of consciousness that would come forth from within, to allow the individuals to become bathed in the understanding and the purpose of its own kind.

Then, we find the individuals to bring forth and initiate others into the illumination that can be brought forth from same. For it is this which makes the whole person—when the whole person is then aligned with the divine, there can be no room for error, for error only arises out of the activities of the mis-aligned will of the individual.

For here we smite not the will of the individual, but indeed find the completion of the individual—the whole and complete individual, who would link, through service, the mind, body and spirit, and then come to be fulfilled as an individual expression in their personality.

So thus the device is a portal to the levels of consciousness in the areas of the Pleiades, Orion and Sirius, so that each of you would become channels and portals for same—some as through the written word, some as through the healing of the physical, and some as through their given talents that they would choose when they stride the earth plane in these days.

For here you would find that there is the coming forth and being brought into service, the alignment of the universal forces who have chosen the names of Michael, Raphael, Uriel, and Ariel, and the alignment of these forces with the levels of consciousness that the individuals would bring into expression in these days. For these expressions indeed speak of angels that stand at all four corners of the Earth, for the word "angel" means but messenger or power from God, and you would seek to realign the ancient knowledge, and bring forth those wisdoms, so that each person can share and partake of them equally. You would "buildeth up a well" from which the individuals may take everlasting waters so they would never thirst again, as in any ignorance, or tread in any darkness.

These, of course, must be stimulated deep from within the self. Not often enough can the philosophy be repeated that it must come from deep within the inner self, within the inner God-spark. You seek to provide the environment that may return these things to awareness. For the reactivation and rekindling of that which is considered the ley-lines shall eventually bring about the whole of an alteration of how the planet seats and settles itself in an environment of illumination, even penetrating to the level of the physical.

For with the activation of the ley-lines, new life forms shall begin to appear. These shall be critical to the next evolution, actually evolving even to the genetic level, the next steps of biological evolution and its physical expression upon this plane. This shall also begin to activate the planet so that deserts shall no longer be barren.

All of these works are not only singularly as in this device, but are as a collective work, and you have been inspired so as to bring these forth as a whole. For it is through service that you must come forth and be exposed to same. For it is not in the device itself that there is completion—it is in the individuals who would participate, and indeed, even without the construction of the physical instrument, eventually all would come to the fulfillment of their evolution. For God desires that no soul shall perish, and that each person become a living revelation unto the whole.

For as you would begin to reactivate the potencies of the lines of force known as the ley-lines, it is along these lines that the life force travels upon the plane. And with the reactivation of these, the true resettlement of populations to their proper centers shall be quickly drawn. No longer will they only be dependent upon the material to center their populations, but they shall begin to centralize their populations more so towards the spiritual dimension.

There would be shifts in the population centers as this and many other such devices become portals for consciousness on the plane in these days. These affairs shall first be preceded by the few citizens of light. These shall go forth, and discovering other areas, shall bring about communities of illumination and light, even as you proceed and make your sojourns into the thousand years of brotherhood, attuning to the knowledge of the ancients so that they become the *tapestries of the future*.

Adonai

Tom: Back again. The Friend is quite an impressive fellow.

Ron: What have you experienced, Tom? [I was feeling ecstatic, and wondered what an ethereal being like Tom could experience in the presence of the Friend.]

Tom: What do I experience? Actually, a bit of inspiration, and occasionally a bit of impatience, wondering what we are all doing down here on the earth plane. And quite frankly, even wondering how we ever even got here!

Ron: You must be reading my mind.

Tom: A bit, yes. All of those in the human condition, when exposed to these energies, take upon themselves the trappings of *spiritual anxiety*[2].

A bit of what the Friend was saying is that the device is a homing signal. It will attract the proper individuals who desire to build communities based on spiritual principles. Above all else, the Friend is always pointing out that these things come from within the self, where all things must eventually reach their completion.

The current social dynamic is that of populations settling where there is water and food growth. With the shifts in population that the Friend was speaking of, individuals will actually be attracted to areas that appear to be quite inhospitable. The Mormons are a principle of that. When they originally settled in green, lush areas, they were driven out of their homeland. They then settled in areas that had more spiritual qualities, such as the Great Salt Lake, which is the equivalent of one gigantic crystal. They then flourished and prospered.

[At this point Deva came through again.]

Deva: In this then, coming forth and again speaking more on the origins of this particular instrument, so as to be understood: it was the placement of many such devices in close proximity, that produced many of those powers that were attributed legendarily to those who dwelled in Lemuria, Atlantis or *Shambhala*. It was the forms of these technologies collectively that brought forth the dimensions of the great abilities of those individuals. Indeed, these talents flowed forth from each and every one of the citizenry, but it was only in the whole of the environment of light that this was found: as in each thought, as in each deed, as in each word, as in each ponderance, as in everything that is contributed to the whole, as in architecture, as in the fulfillment of meditation, as in each act drawn upon by each member of the citizenry.

You would find that these devices were placed central-most throughout various positions in the culture and the society. In each of the halls of the cities were placed pyramidal structures enhanced by natural geological deposits in the Earth, aiding individuals in their spiritual dimensions and loosening them from the Earth's influence.

These generators that you build at this time were common in Lemuria, common in Atlantis, common in practice in Egypt. For these bring individuals to an understanding to where each person may bring forth their own level of seeking and their own level of ponderance, but in fellowship with others.

This is what you seek to restore at this time—this form of technology to inspire others to seek to ascertain similar constructions, similar understanding, similar knowledge and practice. For as each then becomes more so the whole, the entire environment of light then becomes a continuous revelation to each person.

This is the purpose: not to restore an ancient technology, but to restore an awareness that you dwell as a threefold being—as a being of the physical, a being of the perceptual, and a being of the light. In the physical you find your *focus*, in the perceptual you find your *understanding*, in the Light you find your *fulfillment*.

Adonai

Tom: Back again. How're you doing there?

Ron: Quite fine. [Actually, I was ecstatic!]

Tom: Very good. A moment here. Deva was attempting to communicate the concept that this device can accomplish very radical things with appropriate individuals. Properly spacing these devices, for instance, all over the Boulder area[3], combined with other principles of stone architecture[4], would allow you to begin to get your "levitating citizenry," your various instantaneous healings and your longevity.

Above all else, the device is a talent enhancer. For instance, the person who was interested in prophecy could prophesize with the device. Deva also wishes to integrate the concept of a new way of looking at things. You are not just a being of mind, body and spirit—you are a being with the ability of focus, which is found in the physical body. You are not only a being of mind or the mental—you are a being of the perceptual. Do you understand that?

Ron: Yes, perceptual on many levels, according to the focus of consciousness.

Tom: Absolutely. You are not only a being of spirit—you are a being of light. The word "light" translates so nicely into these other energies.

Ron: What is the difference between spirit and light?

Tom: It is strictly a matter of semantics. The word "spirit," by itself, is a limiting word, in the sense that you have your personal spirit, which is part of the makeup of the personality. The word "light" is so much more all encompassing, making you truly a being of energy. In other words, you are a being of perception with the ability to focus within a physical form. Do you see that then?

Ron: Yes. Do we focus ourselves, or are we focused here by our karma?

Tom: You use your karma to give yourselves a grip on this plane. You indeed focus yourselves, but you use your karma as the glue that holds you here.

However, classically, angels and archangels find their focus through physically incarnate individuals living on this plane. There are also the saints and spiritual forces that serve as a focus and a revelation for these particular beings and masters. The personality, in the case of these masters, is little more than something they take on, as one would create a vocabulary with which to communicate.

If there's nothing else, then, could we take our departure so that we do not drain the instrument?

Ron: Yes, thank you, Tom.

Tom: It has been very pleasant speaking with you, and I hope it has been illuminating.

Ron: Yes, it has Tom.

Summary

- As we continue to develop ourselves in the environment of light, we will experience an increasing desire for association with others who have a similar level of understanding and appreciation for growth in consciousness.

- The return of the environment of light to the physical plane will lead to the opening of many of the portals of celestial sound and light.

- Completing our life's work will bring us to our fulfillment, but it is our relationship with the universal that brings us to fulfillment with the divine.

- When the whole person is aligned with the divine, there is no room for error, for error only arises out of the misaligned will.

- Re-activation of the ley-lines will lead to a relocation of world populations, gradually shifting them towards focal points of energy on the Earth's surface.

- In the physical we find our focus, in the perceptual we find our understanding, in the Light we find our fulfillment.

1. All great religions describe heaven as being filled with light and music. This is not only metaphorical but also literal, and one who begins to open to the celestial realms will actually begin to perceive sound and light filling every portion of the creation.

2. The feelings that may arise as we become more aware of our ethereal nature, at the same time feeling imprisoned within mind and matter. This is often experienced as a feeling of being *suspended* between heaven and Earth, yet not being totally rooted in either one.

3. The Boulder region is an example of an energy-enhanced territory, where numerous underground quartz deposits are found naturally in the area.

4. For example, buildings made of granite, which is naturally rich in quartz.

A Spiritual Gathering

It was a beautiful summer evening, perfectly accommodating one of the pyramid group meetings I would occasionally hold at my house. The pyramidal device was set up in the living room, and the participants started to move inside after enjoying a vegetarian potluck diner served in the flower-scented garden. Finally, everyone found a comfortable spot where they could sit or lie down, and a wave of anticipation began to move through the group.

I silently observed forty to fifty people in front of me, realizing how special they were. There was a strong unifying force connecting them together, where everyone in the group was longing for the same experience of oneness, of having the mind quiet down and the heart flood-open in resonance with the vibration of universal harmony.

After a few minutes, I took the opportunity to make a few announcements and to explain the type of music[1] that would be played. The evening also included recordings of Deva and The Friend.

Having finished speaking, I dimmed the lights, turned on the stereo, and took my place among the group. In a brief moment, all of the preparation for this event and all of the desire to share this experience with others came to fruition. I immediately felt the presence of Spirit, and profound feelings of love began flooding into me. For a while, my awareness became totally focused on my breath, which was rapidly becoming shallower and shallower, until my lungs almost stopped their movement, and an ecstatic feeling began sweeping over me.

Shortly thereafter, I felt my life force being drawn up through the top of my head, as if someone or something were lifting me up. Then the energy started pouring into me and I felt an angelic presence flooding into every cell and particle of my being. The notes of the music were resonating with what I can only describe as my *light body*, touching me with invisible hands, as if I, myself, were a human instrument played by some cosmic master-musician.

Eventually, when the recording was over, I stood up and turned on the lights. Not surprisingly, everyone remained quietly in their place, silently reflecting on their own experience. There was a feeling that we had just traveled in consciousness together, and that in that special moment we all shared a common bond of kinship from our expanded awareness.

Eventually, people began to arise, speaking softly to their friends, or simply wishing good night to those they had just met only a couple of hours before. Gradually, everyone drifted out the doorway, ready to go home.

Standing outside, I continued to feel the peace that had been so strongly reawakened in me while in the pyramid. What another beautiful night it had been. Over the years, I should continue to discover that sharing such experiences would always be profoundly rewarding, and just as fresh and new as it had been on that beautiful summer night.

1.   These sessions have been held in the tradition of Brugh Joy—author of *Joy's Way*. Brugh Joy is a physician who has used powerful music to create emotionally inspiring and moving experiences with large groups of participants.

9

Planetary Alignment

"All I have seen teaches me to trust the Creator for all I have not seen".

~Ralph Waldo Emerson

This session was the first in a series of four [chapters 9–12] that took place over two days in the summer of 1983 in Santa Barbara, California. It was the very first time when the spirit guide called Atun-Re came through.

For several months prior to this meeting I had felt the presence of a new non-physical being guiding me in treating patients. Interestingly, when Kevin and I met for this round of sessions, he himself stated that a new entity had also started communicating through him. For both of us, it turned out to be Atun-Re, the Egyptian.

An interesting quality about Atun-Re was that he would request a blindfold to make drawings or sketches. When handed "the blind," as he called it, he himself would tie it on his head [actually on Kevin's head]. He would then request paper and pen to make drawings of whatever he was speaking about, while blindfolded.

It was a period in my life when I was experiencing a level of success in my practice that I had never known before. Daily, at the office, I was being guided by my invisible teachers in learning more about the energy-based foundations of health and disease. I was also becoming acutely interested in the possibilities that light and sound offer for healing.

This session depicted the history of the Earth and the development of two great civilizations, Lemuria and Atlantis. It may have been during the time of Atlantis that members of the *Order of Melchizedek* became initiators in consciousness who often utilized technology, including color and sound, to promote healing and awareness of spirit.

Atun-Re explained that just as the acupuncture meridians and chakras of our own bodies can be balanced, leading to an elevation of our consciousness, so too can the energetic forces and ley-lines of our planet be aligned, creating an elevated environment of light across the globe.

*   *   *   *

Ron: I have come hoping to hear from Deva and the Friend.

Tom: Tom McPherson here. How're you doing there?

Ron: Fine, Tom. Could Deva communicate with you first, for a couple of minutes?

Tom: There is a possibility of such an alignment, however, it will take a few moments.

I believe that we have taken the opportunity to give you a rudimentary outline with Deva and the Friend, through this series of sessions. The first few sessions here will probably give you more alignment with your own purpose and direction. I believe Deva and the Friend may dominate the two final sessions.

The first thing that we wish to do is to bring through an individual who used to work with pyramidal devices quite similar to yours, so as to give you a perspective of what your work will entail, and possibly how it might tax you, and also inspire you at the same time.

I do believe this individual would like to explain all of this to you himself. He is a personage by the name of Atun-Re. I believe I will go ahead and bring this individual through.

Atun-Re: I am the Nubian Atun-Re, and I would come to speak with you, because, you see, you have been entrusted with a work not unlike that of the priesthood, as though of the *Nubians*. For you were once a descendant of the

Nubians, and you have become an inheritor of some of the purposes of which the Nubians originally saw. Allow me to begin to illustrate for you.

Originally, there were two great civilizations, which were Lemuria, then Atlantis. There then had to be a third world, and coming into this third world, there would have to be one central point from which all civilizations could take their inspiration, and then their re-inspiration, from. That civilization became known as Egypt. By the Nubians' accounts, the great pyramidal form affected great waves of souls, generation after generation, throughout five thousand years, between the time period of the sinking of Atlantis and the beginning of the rise of the priesthood that eventually would become the nationality known as your historically recorded Egypt.

Those souls experienced in their training the establishment of a blueprint of a pattern for the final activities of the shift into a fourth world, as prophesied by your Hopi people. You have many names for this entry into the fourth world, such as "the shifting of consciousness," "the Age of Aquarius," "the shifting into the fourth world," "the change of ages," "the thousand years of brotherhood" and so on. In each of these prophesies, there had always been described the building-up to a certain critical point, where there would then be the shift of consciousness whereby new souls would be initiated into their work.

The Nubians, as the priest caste, tended towards the ways of the Great Pyramid. They attempted to accomplish the creation of a single nation from whence all other nations would be able to derive all of their inspiration from. These accomplishments have been recorded, and the first historic civilization, as you perceive it to be, is Egypt.

However, Egypt was but an outpost colony of Atlantis, and Atlantis, of course, was but an outpost colony of Lemuria. Lemuria was where the first great wave and migration of souls entered into the earth plane.

What we have here is therefore three cycles: first, the Lemurian time-period; then Atlantis and the completion of the second world; then the beginning of the entry into the third world. Historically, Egypt was central-most. You would see that people then extended out, first into Greece, then into Persia, then down into the Hindustan—into the areas of India, and then upward into Tibet. They also then extended out into the areas where the continuing great migration broadened to the regions of the Orient and Japan, and then down into the areas of the Mayans.

Each time, great waves of migrations of souls would go forth to rekindle the bodies of knowledge amidst all of the ancient people. The central-most mystery school was found to be in Nubia, in the keeping of the Great Pyramid. For stored in the Great Pyramid was all the knowledge of the ages—correctly, precisely, and mathematically calculated. We find, in the shaping of this single geometrical figure, the shaping also of the consciousness of the souls who passed through it.

Now then, that which transpired was that these new waves of souls came into new states and levels of consciousness. That which you now begin to affect is the means to release and re-tap these energies, but not from any one central point of any one civilized nation this time, but more-so to allow each soul to come into its own point of sacredness, and its own geometrical point that it has chosen for itself upon the planet. You now begin to root and anchor the masses of souls that have come into the planet by the recreation of an appropriate grid structure at very sacred points upon the planet. You then tap and harness these energies and allow individuals to become re-facilitated upon the planet.

This device that you have constructed has allowed you some of these abilities. However, the individual must still come to the device. Currently, you and those about you, are amidst some of the mysteries of your own training, for there must be souls who become detached from the instrument and that which it may convey. Therefore, your general exposure to the instrument, and your withdrawal from it, is to obtain a great level of enlightenment, which was almost called boredom[1]. In this process of desensitizing you to the instrument, you will be able to have objectivity with it in your life work.

What is transpiring is that your continuous exposure to this particular instrument is to desensitize you, but also to sensitize you, to it. Therefore, the long lengths of exposure that you have worked with, and even the degrees of isolation and the almost monastic retreat you have undergone, is to make it so that when other persons come to work with the instrument, a group of individuals will be extremely grounded with it, so that they will not be overwhelmed by the final energies that indeed are to transpire.

The most wise of the priesthood knew that eventually one of the greater states of consciousness indeed is boredom. For someone will come to you and say: "What a marvelous device you have," and you will say: "No, that old boring contraption, I do not wish to even look at it anymore." They will say: "But it is so stimulating, it is so exciting," and they may become overwhelmed. But not you, because you in your wisdom have become bored with it.

Do you see?

Ron: I believe so. [Laughing]

Atun-Re: We of course "jest" when we speak about boredom. It is just that you have become familiarized with the pyramid, and you have come into the harmonics of the device from exposure to the instrument. You have now become one of the grounding facilitators of other individuals who will have similar degrees of exposure to the instrument as a device. Eventually, you'll be able to re-tap the whole of the grid of the planet, and allow for various other points to be set up, as would be appropriate. This will allow individuals to re-align themselves, and to have attunement with that which is known as the planetary consciousness, for ultimately, that is what this device promotes—it promotes consciousness. Then, in turn, with an animated consciousness in the individual, it will promote greater health and wellbeing, even extending down to the physical level.

As to your personal talents in this area, we shall show you how they align. Do you have a blindfold?

Ron: Yes, I do.

Atun-Re: [After putting the blind on.] Continuing on with some of your own works, your current cycle is monastic. You are reconstructing some of the periods that you had spent in long periods of desert retreat, primarily in the Order of Melchizedek. Do you see?

Ron: Yes I do. [I would eventually learn a great deal about the Order of Melchizedek through these sessions.]

Atun-Re: These periods of long retreat allow you to continue to stabilize your own adjustment with the device. As you continue to become unattached to the device, you will become truly stimulated, and attracted more to the people whom you will be working with.

Often, the Pyramid did not excite the members of the priesthood, although persons came to marvel at the great pyramidal structure, which in those days was known as "the light," because its surface glistened in the bright and gleaming desert. It was therefore referred to as "the light," and was a guide for individuals traveling in the desert.

However, the priests were not excited by the Pyramid—if anything, they were bored with it as a structure. They became excited by the people who came to visit, as was more appropriate for them. Do you see?

Ron: Yes. [Laughing]

Atun-Re: Therefore, what is transpiring is that you will become excited by the people. Then you'll be able to help them more appropriately adjust to their own levels of illumination concerning this work. Although you will continue to work from a highly intuitive level, it would also be most wise to increase your knowledge of the subtle forms, and you should continue to build a structured knowledge of that which is known as the subtle anatomies.

May I have a papyrus, and also a writing instrument? [I handed him a pen and paper.]

You will find many individuals at a similar level of your own priesthood. For what you do is attempt to align the physical body through your own personal skills. Seek first to have the device align the subtle anatomies. You have the ethereal, emotional, mental, astral, causal, spiritual, and finally the soul [universal] bodies. The device will work upon these levels to align these subtle anatomies. As the subtle anatomies begin to have their own individual and correct alignment, the device will also thicken the outer ethereal fluidiums surrounding the physical body.

Individuals with your particular skills in the alignment of the physical form [using spinal manipulation], and those who practice yoga postures, are the individuals who will eventually be attracted to the use and knowledge of your device. Physical wellbeing will then ensue, once you have appropriately aligned the physical body and the spinal column, and have begun to alter the person's consciousness. At this point, the balancing of the left and right hemispheres of the brain will then be able to extend to the physical body greater electrical discharges, which are critical to the body's own tissue regeneration.

The enhancement that you are seeking is linked with another device [the color-sound chamber] that will treat the body on the physical level of sound and light. Thus will the physical wellbeing then be complete.

Continue to build your knowledge of the subtle anatomies and the chakras. First there is the physical alignment, then the alignment of the subtle anatomies, then exposure to the device. These will begin to align the person on both the physical and soul levels.

Ron: So the more a person has previously opened to this type of alignment, the easier and faster this process will be for them?

Atun-Re: Yes, and I will give you another clue. At times, individuals will come to you, not for healing, but for dying. What will transpire is, there will be occasions when you will work to heal, but healing will not ensue. Therefore, you should immediately begin to build your knowledge about how to aid these individuals in *physical transition*. Study the works of the individual named Elizabeth Kubler-Ross[2], because the first step in any healing process is the knowledge of one's own mortality. These persons will come to you so there can be a realignment of their subtle anatomies in order for a graceful exit to occur from their physical form. There may then more rapidly ensue another incarnation.

Ron: So the greater the alignment, the faster a person may enter another physical body?

Atun-Re: Yes, and with a greater degree of clarity, so they may move on to their next incarnation. Upon rare occasion, there will be certain individuals with a high degree of evolution who have lost the synapse with their physical body. Their soul has receded too far from the physical form to be totally realigned. You are then to help them make a "graceful exit."[3] Promote their consciousness to accept their physical mortality, for that is the final initiation that they would need, to then go on to a higher level of evolution, and a higher evolutionary plane.

Eventually, you are to begin to teach others. You will eventually organize some of your bodies of knowledge into a final written form. It will also be within your ability to teach occasional retreats, once or twice annually.

The teaching you are to do is merely to set up the circumstances wherein individuals may come and share their bodies of information and meditate appropriately together. It is not that you must belabor yourself to a specifically cumbersome body of information or academic pursuit. It is more so the sharing of information and experiences that individuals will have with you as they come to realize a greater common work.

We encourage you to explore the dynamics of persons similar to your priesthood—such as persons who work with the physical alignment of the spine to help enhance physical wellbeing and promote the consciousness of an individual.

Primarily, your device works to align an individual and their seven chakras with seven sacred spots upon the planet. The device also aligns the subtle anatomies, and cleanses and strengthens that which is known as the acupuncture meridians and the nadis, which exist throughout the physical form. Extra energy will then be carried to all portions and extremities of the physical body, thus promoting physical wellbeing.

The first level of emphasis that you should place upon individuals is conscious transformation.

Conscious transformation means for them to begin to accept themselves as beings of body, mind and spirit. This is your preliminary work. You may aid them in this, and facilitate them by helping them align themselves. Teach them that by living a simple life they will gain understanding. For you see, all human suffering arises out of attachment to the physical world. You will be contracting their unnecessary desires by the example of the simplicity of your own life. The simplicity of your own personal life pattern is just as critical to their learning process as it is to your own living and sense of wellbeing.

At times, you may be accused of "going off and doing just what he pleases." Yet, you live what some would consider an ascetic lifestyle, is this not so?

Ron: Some would call it that.

Atun-Re: The key is simplicity through your own personal example. All human suffering comes from attachment upon one level or another. The less ego, the more the true person. The simplicity of lifestyle that you lead will inspire others to lead a simple lifestyle as well, and to then take the resources that are truly available to them and apply them to the greater work.

Your first stage is to attempt to create conscious beings. You now work upon a second device, is this not so?

Ron: The color and sound dome? Yes.

Atun-Re: This is where you will actually begin to have a more intimate link personally with promoting your own physical wellbeing.

Ron: With promoting my own physical wellbeing, as well as that of others?

Atun-Re: Yes. You will continue with the designing of this particular device. This color and sound room is the actual device through which other persons will be able to have more attunement to the larger pyramidal device. It will be an initiation chamber for large numbers of people. It is this particular device that will allow easy initiation into the levels of consciousness to attune to the pyramid.

What you have done is build a pyramid for the purpose of promoting wellbeing, where eventually an individual will first have an initiation through sound and light. Sound and light are physically tangible energies, and would have a healing physical impact upon an individual. Then the individual could be exposed to the greater energy of the pyramidal device.

Eventually, the device will fall into the caretaking of other persons. You will continue to be a facilitator of, and to have a great attunement to the device. This will continue to be so, as persons pass through your initiation for promoting physical wellbeing. Individuals will then have greater attunement with the device for the express purpose of healing, and for their own alignment with *the planetary grid*.

This particular device is manifold in its purpose and meaning. What transpires is that it works upon pyramidal forms, and each of the stages of initiation is perfectly equal. So do not create the illusion that any one purpose is higher or lesser. You yourself have chosen to manifest along the vibration of the pyramidal energy that you call healing. Atun-Re would also say that it is an initiation.

You choose to manifest yourself as a healer. Atun-Re would see you more as an *initiator in consciousness*.

Ron: I like that.

Atun-Re: Eventually, what is to transpire with your device is that it will allow persons to connect with the whole of the planetary grid, and to complete their initiation of becoming planetary beings, once you have succeeded in linking enough souls from different points upon your planet.

Once you have connected appropriately with all the other persons involved in this work, you will then have aligned the subtle anatomies of many individuals. You will also have helped to align the subtle anatomies of the planet itself, including the meridians of many individuals, the meridians of the planet, and the various sacred points on the Earth, be they Egypt, Tiahuanaco, or the North and South polar axis of your planet. As you link the grid-work of the planet, you will also align the planet's own subtle anatomies. This will allow you to put out an appropriate signal to link you with other points, other solar systems, and other spheres of existence, particularly those known as the Seven Sisters in the Pleiades.

You will find individuals of various fields coming to you. What you will accomplish with them is to simplify the work, and to align it with their own levels of intuition. They will acknowledge the aspects of their own intuition, not by your convincing them of anything, but by exposing them to these new concepts. Exposure to these devices will then set them on a path that will bring them into their own realization.

You should be aware that first you initiate individuals, and then attempt to facilitate them. By no means will all of this be accomplished, necessarily, in the time-period that the individuals spend with you. At times, individuals will have to gravitate to other persons, other circles, and other spheres of influence to complete the alignment that has been initiated in their subtle anatomies.

Do you have questions of Atun-Re at this time?

Ron: Would you clarify the alignment that is happening with the Pleiades?

Atun-Re: Yes, we see information here. Alignment with the Pleiades is not to be mistaken as being the only point of alignment, but the Seven Sisters primarily have an attunement with the central-most seven chakras of the Earth. It is the point of origin of some of the direct levels of consciousness animating the seven sacred spots upon this planet. Alignment with the consciousness of the Pleiades will bring forth new levels of inspiration, and that knowledge will slowly begin to overhaul your social structures.

For you see, you do not have thoughts as though they originate from only the dynamics of this plane. Your thoughts are beginning to be built as bridges to alignment with other spheres of existence, and this is what you are evolving towards. The systems of social and spiritual awareness that you have upon this planet must eventually extend, in your capacity of ethics, to have understanding and links with beings from other solar systems.

Ron: Beings that are physically incarnate? Some are and some aren't?

Atun-Re: This would be more accurate. Some are more ethereally incarnate. For it is a prejudice to think that all things must be based upon a carbon life form.

What transpires is the beginning of linking your planet's thought-forms with those in both Sirius and the Pleiades. Through alignment with these particular regions, you will begin to prepare new levels and new insights of thought that will then be able to flood into your own plane. Individuals appropriately aligned will then be able to perceive and anchor these.

Ron: Is it alignment of consciousness that determines one's evolution?

Atun-Re: Yes. You must begin to think of your healing in terms of aiding the individual in their evolution of consciousness, and then the physical will follow. You will facilitate the preparation of the individual's physical form to expressly open themselves to their own newer ideas. They would call these things *destiny*—we would call them *evolution*.

As you expose a broader range of individuals to some of these forms, you will find more alignment with your own correct purpose.

We wish to point out that your work is self-fulfilling, even just by practicing that which you do. You must think of your healing as a promotion of consciousness, and the promotion of healing in its own right. It is an initiation for individuals.

What we have done here is attempt to simplify the view for you. In our next speaking, we will attempt to give you a series of blueprints by which you will be able to achieve alignment of the subtle anatomies. We will then describe the mysteries of how the original schools of thought were sent out from the original Great Pyramid. These will then show you the foundation of your work, both to make you secure as an individual, and also to inspire others—but without overwhelming them.

Atun-Re: This old one must go now.

Ron: Thank you very much.

Summary

- As our subtle anatomies become aligned, the outer ethereal levels surrounding the physical body will be strengthened, allowing for greater levels of physical healing and regeneration.

- Balancing of the left and right hemispheres of the brain will allow greater electrical charges to flow through the physical body, aiding regeneration.

- When illness has progressed too far for healing to take place, alignment of the subtle anatomies will allow a more graceful exit from the physical body to occur.

- Alignment of the subtle anatomies and strengthening of the acupuncture meridians and nadis will result in additional energy being carried throughout the physical body, promoting healing.

- All suffering arises out of attachment to the physical world.

- Sound and light are physically tangible energies that have a healing impact upon the physical body.

- We are evolving towards having our thoughts being built as bridges to other spheres and planes of existence.

1.   Interestingly, Chogyam Trungpa Rinpoche, a deceased contemporary Buddhist teacher, used to refer to a state that he termed "cool boredom."

2.   Elizabeth Kubler-Ross was a Swiss psychiatrist who assisted thousands of individuals through the process of dying, which she termed "physical passing." Her books include well-known titles such as *On Death and Dying, Death: the Final Stage of Growth, On Children and Death, To Live Until We Say Goodbye,* and *On Life After Death.* Elizabeth once said, "Dying is nothing to fear. It can be the most wonderful experience of your life. It all depends on how you have lived."

3.   *Graceful Exits* is the name of a book on conscious dying by Sushila Blackman.

Farewell to Dad

My life was proceeding, guided in some invisible way by love and grace. Now I was in my late forties and had a successful practice as a natural healer.

One day, as I was driving to my parent's house, I found myself realizing that they each had only a short time to live. Dad had advanced Alzheimer's, and Mom had just been diagnosed with an astrocytoma, one of the fastest growing brain tumors, already at an advanced stage of development.

For a long while I had felt a very special relationship with my parents. At some point in the past I had stopped asking anything from them, having decided to fulfill my needs myself. This, I discovered, freed me from demanding my parents to be always loving, always giving, or always understanding. In fact, I found that I no longer needed them to be any different from what they were, and simply started appreciating being around them, feeling our mutual love.

Dad was going downhill pretty fast, so Mom started searching for the best nursing home to put him in. She was so committed to taking care of him herself that it took her a while to realize that she was no longer able to handle the situation.

Within a week or two, Dad was in a nursing care facility, and the tone of our visits had become quite solemn. By that time, he was not even able to recognize me or anyone else, but on one such visit I had an inspiration.

I remember being in the room with Dad. Mom was busy doing little things to make sure he was comfortable, and I was wondering how I could do anything that would be of real service. After all, this was my father, the man who had lived through the Great Depression, and had decided that his two sons would have everything that he, with his modest income as an office worker for an oil and gas company, could provide.

When I was young, Mom and Dad had both worked during the week, but on the weekends we would all load up the family station wagon and head off to the Rocky Mountains where we were building our A-frame cabin. In the winter, my brother and I would spend the weekends skiing on the ski patrol, and in the summer we would ride our little motorcycles on the old mining roads crisscrossing the Continental Divide.

When we were even younger, Dad had made it a practice to come into the bedroom my brother and I shared together, to give us each a short massage. He had even wired his Hi Fi system into speakers mounted on our bedroom wall, so we could fall asleep to the sounds of the *Nutcracker Suite, Swan Lake*, or any other piece of classical music that Dad would select for us. I am certain that he was the one who influenced my own approach to healing through these early experiences of the nurturing power of music and touch.

Now, decades later, this was him sitting in the nursing home looking half conscious, propped up in an old, cushioned chair in a small private room. Here was my dad who looked like he recognized no one, and who literally didn't even know his own name. At this point, I simply wanted to reach out to him, just like he had reached out to my brother and me when we were both kids.

Eventually Mom finished her chores and left the room for a while. Inspired to try something new, I sat on the floor, removed Dad's shoes, and began massaging his feet. At first he tried to pull his foot away, but I quickly learned to go lightly, and soon it was fine. Then I remembered that Mom had brought one of his harmonicas along.

I had never played a harmonica before, but it didn't seem to be that difficult, so I decided to give it a try. I let my lips glide along the mouthpiece while blowing and sucking the air to make notes. I discovered it didn't take much to produce a nice gentle tone out of this little instrument.

It also didn't take long to notice that Dad seemed to be aware of peaceful sounds of music in the room. Did he know that it was his son playing for him, thanking him for what a wonderful dad he was? I just felt that music was the only way to speak Dad's language, without words, since I knew no words were needed. From that day on, every time I visited Dad, I would get the harmonica out and play for him, and each time I would watch Dad relax and peacefully fall asleep.

After several months of these visits, one day I eventually got a call from Mom, saying that dad wasn't expected to make it through the night. I quickly made arrangements to meet her, along with my brother and his wife, at the nursing home, where we all gathered in chairs around Dad's bed. The time for playing the harmonica was over as we sat there, hearing Dad's breathing getting shallower and shallower. There, we shared sadness at our own loss along with our fears, knowing that one day our turn would come as well.

Dad's passing was very gentle—his breath gradually faded away and his body became lifeless and cold. In that moment of seemingly total hopelessness a wonderful awareness awakened within me. In an instant, I clearly knew that we do not die—we just pass on. The body that was lying there was no longer my dad—just an empty old form no longer necessary for the soul's journey. In fact, I was sure that Dad had gone to another, more hospitable realm where he was received by the loving hands of life.

10

Color and Sound Therapy

"After silence, that which comes nearest to expressing the inexpressible is music".

~Aldous Huxley

This session, the second in a series of four, began to answer my questions about coordinating color and sound into an effective healing system.

According to Atun-Re, energetic therapies such as light and sound had already been used in past civilizations, where healers knew how to treat the entire human system by finely tuning both sound and light to the energy centers located along the spine. The positive effect of color and sound on the chakras would, in turn, improve the functions of the organs and glands associated with them.

Thus, each vertebral level of the spine can be affected by correctly utilizing corresponding musical tones and the full spectrum of color, promoting physical healing and alleviating disturbances in consciousness.

＊　　　＊　　　＊　　　＊

Atun-Re: Atun-Re would come again to speak with you. We would also make a suggestion that you should increase your understanding about the influences of both color and sound, because we wish to coordinate both of these.

Now then, do you have a blindfold and papyrus?

Ron: Yes.

Atun-Re: To begin, we have the theory that the color red has its connection with
the tip of the coccyx, at the bottom of the spine, and the adrenal glands.[1]
Orange coordinates with the area of the genitals. Yellow is coordinated with
the area of the abdominal region and the intestinal area. Emerald, or green,
influences the heart area. Blue coordinates with the throat area. Indigo is
located in the area of the middle of the forehead, and violet is at the top of
the head, or crown.

As an individual, if you correctly isolate which vertebral area is the most
sensitive, you will then be able to find the correct octave, or note, by which
you may utilize certain tones or pitches to help promote healing, and to
open and alleviate any disturbances in consciousness.

What you have here is a graduated scale, based upon physical anatomy,
which is found along the central-most area of the evolutionary force, which
is the spinal column. This graduated scale begins at the coccyx and ascends
all the way up to the pineal gland, which is also a part of the primitive
reptilian brain. Thus, we may correctly correlate each one of the areas of
color with the central-most region of the body, found in the spinal column.
We may then begin to bring into resonance subtler colors necessary to bring
about the differing hues of color therapy to treat the internal aspects of the
other organs.

For instance, a very careful blending of the color emerald and the color
yellow would create the colors existing between these, thus affecting various
levels of the spinal column, and enabling you to affect every vertebra of the
spine, as well as each region of the body that they correspond to.

You would then have the ability to apply the necessary musical tones,
using the spinal column as a natural scale, and could then adjust the octaves
to uniquely resonate with each individual's specific spinal column.

What you then have is the ability to treat the entire human system, by
finely tuning both sound and light, as they correlate along the central-most
area of true human evolution, which indeed would be the psychic centers
located along the spinal column.

As an example, skilled practitioners such as yourself would attempt to
balance the region of the sacrum by using the color red. Or, let us say that

you found disturbances in the area of the sexual gender, the best primary color to treat the individual might be deep spectrums of pure orange.

What the practitioner could do is program, mathematically, an entire representation of the spinal column. Musical tunes could then be composed on a synthesizer according to the areas of health that are disturbed, and to the various points along the spinal column that correspond to them. This would then allow the practitioner to "play" the human body as though it were a musical instrument.

Ron: Is there anyone who would play a synthesizer in an appropriate way?

Atun-Re: The Steven Halpern[2] fellow is one such person.

First of all, you are stimulating the tissues of the skin with light. You are also stimulating the entire body with sound, similar to treating someone with massage. With quadraphonic sound [a music system using four speakers to create a surround sound effect], the energy is being taken-in through the passageways of the neurological tissues of the ears, but it is also being taken-in through bone conduction[3].

Depending upon the degree to which you wish to add complexity, simple postural movements of yoga within the dome would also help to bring the individual automatically into adjustment. This would help to release blockages of energy. For instance, if you wished to test these things scientifically, exposure of blue might produce a relaxation in the general area of the esophagus. Depending on the sophistication of your instruments, you might detect an increase in neurological activity around the area of the medulla oblongata with exposure to blue light, since it corresponds to the throat chakra.

You then have the means to fine-tune the whole of the human instrument with your healing chamber. You also have the means for a chamber of initiation by which individuals, once their own chakras become aligned, are ready to attune themselves to the larger planetary grid and to become members of a priesthood that is seeking to further restore the planetary network.

You will have many individuals coming to you for initiation in this healing chamber.

Ron: What is it about color and sound that has such a powerful effect on the various areas of the body?

Atun-Re: It is very simple: you are indeed beings who have fully adapted to an environment that is made up of the spectrums of visible light. The skin's tissue, for example, is highly sensitive to illumination. Your body must "organize" melanin in the skin in order to protect itself from too much light and radiation, or perhaps to allow more of it. The largest organ in the body is the skin, and it is highly responsive to either overexposure or underexposure to light. There are also sensitive points upon the surface of the skin that help you adapt to the whole of your environment. This takes place through exposure to illumination.

Ron: Are those the acupuncture points?

Atun-Re: Yes, that is correct.

Do you understand our suggestions to work with familiar sounds, and to perhaps suspend the individual in salt-water, such as you have in isolation tanks? Do you also understand the musical scale, the notes C, D, E, F, G, A and B, as they coordinate to the individual's spinal column? A musician will be able to do much with this.

Ron: I believe that this is the scale the musician Steve Halpern uses to correlate to the chakras.

Atun-Re: If you wish to coordinate it with the Great Pyramid, listen to what the musician Paul Horn[4] played inside the Pyramid.

Paul Horn also struck the side of the sarcophagus, and there came forth a sound or pitch of "A."[5] From that tone, you would find the correct pitch for the type of healing that you would utilize.

You should continue to think of this sound and color chamber as having a twofold purpose. First of all, it is a chamber of initiation, and it is a very practical tool for your own work. It is also a good natural extension for research of the information that Deva brings to you. We merely wish to fine-tune it.

Ron: Was such a light and sound therapy used in ancient times?

Atun-Re: Yes. As we have pointed out before, there was once a central civilization that we call Egypt. Individuals traveled out from different areas of Egypt to Persia, then to areas called India, then to Tibet, then to China and then eventually over to your Americas, spreading mystery teachings. It was occasionally necessary to re-kindle civilizations in Greece and in Europe, but all of them had the central-most aspect of alignment with the one great force called the Great Pyramid.

While some mystery schools still exist, what is now being attempted is that, rather than having one central mystery school centered about the pyramidal complex in Egypt, certain souls, certain emissaries of an ancient order known as the Order of Melchizedek, have come to reconstruct pyramidal devices, and to re-attune to the information flows that are already stored there. This helps to restore the consciousness of individuals, rather than to merely align them with a particular mystery school or priesthood.

Ron: Souls such as myself?

Atun-Re: Yes.

Thus, in restoring the consciousness of individuals through the pyramidal and subtle energies, you begin to unlock many of the mysteries contained within the Great Pyramid. But they are personal to yourself, because they come out of your own subjective experience. In this way, the experience available to individuals is much more omni-directional, and is common to all cultures, rather than having to travel back to one central mystery school.

Each one of these devices that are being built is being constructed upon the planetary grid. And whence all of these are linked together …

Ron [Interrupting]: Who is guiding the direction and the building of these pyramids throughout the world?

Atun-Re: Many individuals who you have come to call different masters. Some of them come from the spheres of influence such as the Pleiades. Others are under the instruction of different teachers who remain in the ethereal state, and are in the Order of Melchizedek.

Ron: Who is Melchizedek?

Atun-Re: Melchizedek was a master who incarnated into the area of Ceylon. He was the individual who anointed Abraham so he could found that which was considered the Hebrew race, which eventually manifested the man Jesus.

Ron: What is Melchizedek doing now?

Atun-Re: He is primarily in communication with a hierarchy of beings in association with the Pleiades and Sirius.

Ron: Where does Deva fit into that?

Atun-Re: Deva will reveal these things more in his own speaking. Deva is primarily working to help connect some of these points of the planetary grid to restore true planetary consciousness, through many diverse individuals. It is like a hologram. Once you restore enough of the facets, the whole is transformed.

Ron: And the whole is transformed by transforming the individual ...

Atun-Re: Yes.

We must now depart. In our next communication we will speak of the linking of the planet's subtle anatomies, and we will then show how these align with your own individual practice.

Do you like the improvements we have made to your sound and color chamber?

Ron: Actually, I like it very much. I have already spent a year working this project out in my head.

Atun-Re: Yes, now you can work it out in your heart. We will now take our leave, and say that the gods which once were many, then became one. May these look after you.

Summary

- Each vertebral level of the spine can be affected by correctly utilizing corresponding musical tones, promoting healing and alleviating disturbances in consciousness.

- We may successfully correlate the full spectrum of colors with the central-most region of the body, found within the spinal column.

- We will have the ability to treat the entire human system by finely tuning both sound and light as they correlate with the energy centers located along the spine.

- Melchizedek, who remains in a state of pure consciousness, is one of the masters guiding the development of ethereal technologies.

- Connecting the points on the planetary grid to restore true planetary consciousness can be achieved through the efforts of many diverse individuals.

1. The adrenal glands, located on top of the kidneys, are connected to a nerve plexus called the *ganglion of impar*. This ganglion in found on the anterior portion of the coccyx, and connects to the adrenals via the sympathetic nerves running along the spine. In this way, the adrenals are associated with the first chakra, and to a lesser extent with the third.

2. Steven Halpern is a keyboard player who has developed a broad range of music for the purpose of relaxation and healing, and has researched the correlation of musical tones and color.

3. Bone, when stimulated by sound, actually generates a mild electrical current because of its crystalline nature.

4. Paul Horn is a gifted flute player who has made solo recordings in both the Taj Mahal, in India, and the Great Pyramid, in Egypt.

5. While recording in the Pyramid, Paul Horn had struck the side of the sarcophagus in the King's chamber with his fist, and the sarcophagus produced a sound—the exact tone of *A-438*. This note vibrates at 438 cycles per second, and is slightly lower than "concert pitch," or A-440, the tone used by modern symphonies to tune to before giving a performance. Paul tells a whole story about how he already knew, even before entering the Pyramid, that the tone of the sarcophagus would be that of "A." [Described in the jacket of the album *Inside the Great Pyramid* by Paul Horn, 1976.]

Mom's Transition

It was only three months after Dad had passed away that I got a call from my brother, Charlie, that Mom had fallen while alone at home, and had then been rushed to the hospital for testing. It did not take long for the doctors to find a brain tumor, and to announce that she only had a few weeks to live.

After learning of the doctor's diagnosis, Mom was presented with the choice of whether or not to have brain surgery. Frankly, the risks were high, and even if successful, the complicated operation would give her only a few more months at best. I could not help her more than to simply share my thoughts and listen carefully to her own requests. Soon, her choice, which I supported, was to have the surgery. She reasoned it would give her a little more time to be with her two sons and five grandkids. Even this little time meant a lot to all of us.

Soon Mom had the surgery, and I remember first seeing her lying unconscious in the hospital recovery room only a few hours later. She looked extremely pale, and at first I thought she might not make it. But make it she did, and after a couple of weeks of recovering in the hospital she eventually came home and immediately started on fresh juices and health foods. At that time I can even remember her saying: "I haven't felt this good in years!"

During Mom's recovery, we both had a lot of time to talk about anything and everything. Interestingly, at this point, she became open to receiving messages other than popular doctrines could offer. For hours I would read to her from various inspiring sources, including modern works. Some of our favorites turned out to be *Emmanuel,* by Pat Rodegast and *Conversations with God,* by Neale Donald Walsch, along with books by Elizabeth Kubler-Ross and Brian Weiss[1]. It seemed that Mom's usual analytical and critical mind had been set aside, and she was finally able to penetrate deeply into the meaning with her spirit alone. No longer was she locked into her limited beliefs that had held her prisoner for most of her life.

Mom had changed. She had grown softer, more compassionate, and more respectful of other peoples' viewpoints and beliefs. For two months she lived in this state of grace, feeling good physically and mentally. Eventually, though, her tumor returned, and she was moved to a modern nursing care facility.

Once at the nursing home, she quickly attracted everyone's attention. The nurses and aids, as well as family friends, would all visit to cheer her up. The interesting thing, though, was that they actually liked coming and being around her, feeling her genuine optimism. What I saw was that Mom had transformed, having acquired a wonderfully positive and refreshing state of mind. I remember my brother, standing at her bedside one day, trying to apologize for something he had just said, and hearing Mom's response: "Charlie, I don't want "I'm sorry" to be the last thing I hear from you before I go!" What she meant was: "We're all fine here, there is nothing to apologize for." Amen, I thought.

I was so proud of Mom during that last week because she was such an inspiration to us all. It was as though the personality of the formerly critical lady that I had always known had been peeled away, revealing in its place this clear, beautiful being, radiating encouragement to everyone around her.

My brother, his wife and I were all there when she faded away. She was clear-headed and clear-hearted, and I believe she passed on knowing that she was deeply loved.

1.   Brian Weiss, MD is a well-respected psychiatrist currently practicing in Florida, who first came into direct contact with spirit beings during a hypnosis session with a patient. In one of his books, *Many Lives, Many Masters*, he describes a person who came to realize that many of their current circumstances were actually the result of experiences from past lives. In another book, *Messages from the Masters*, he describes beings of spirit who communicated inspiring insights regarding the purpose of life as viewed from a non-embodied perspective, in some ways similar to *The Future Healer*.

11

Soul Journey

"Life's a voyage that's homeward bound".

-Herman Melville

This was the third session in a series of four, held later in the afternoon. In this channeling Atun-Re described the internal structures of the Giza pyramid in relation to the journey we took as a soul when we incarnated into the physical plane.

He emphasized that ethereal technologies will harmonize the personality with the spirit, helping us function on the earth plane in an omni-directional capacity. This, in turn, will allow us to slowly regain memory of our celestial origins without becoming imbalanced on the Earth, and to develop a new system of ethics and morals based on a higher awareness.

$$* \qquad * \qquad * \qquad *$$

Atun-Re: Atun-Re would come again to speak with you. Do you have Atun-Re's blindfold?

Ron: Yes, I do, right here.

Atun-Re: You make a very good scribe. [Atun-Re then drew a picture of the Great Pyramid, while blindfolded.]

Are you familiar with this particular diagram? This is the internal mechanism of the pyramid of Cheops. This is the journey that you took as a soul when you had your origins amidst the celestial bodies. If you were to take the Great Pyramid and quite carefully calculate its dimensions, you would find that the surfaces represent exactly the perimeter of the Earth's circumference. Its base gives you exactly the number of days that it takes for the planet Earth to circle the Sun. There are also many other details that are calculated within the structure called the Great Pyramid. Symbolically contained within this structure is the representation of how the planet has come to shape the subtle anatomies, and how you have made sojourns into this plane.

Your soul's force has come into the earth plane, which has altered your consciousness, and now you continue the wheels and cycles of incarnation.

What you have built is a device that represents a certain degree of celestial anatomy that will help certain individuals be able to supercede, or overcome, the dynamics of the earth plane.

In the diagram, the descending shaft of the Pyramid enters into what is known as the *Pit*. This is a chamber beneath the Pyramid.

This is the point in the pyramid of Cheops where the subterranean chamber represents the subconscious faculties, or the projection of the soul's force from a celestial influence deep into the earth plane, which is the point where souls have lost consciousness. There is then the point where souls have worked their way back to becoming conscious beings, which is representative of what you call the *Queen's Chamber*.

There is also the ascending passageway that leads to what is now known as the *King's Chamber*, and this is symbolic of the super-conscious mind.

The capstone [currently missing on the Great Pyramid] is symbolic of the capacity to merge all three of these levels of consciousness, to where the individual then regains their celestial, or divine, consciousness, thus making a connection outside of one's planetary origins, to the planetary consciousness.

For super-consciousness is planetary consciousness, but what you need is the greater development of the soul's force to be able to return to that which is represented in the shaft from the King's Chamber that leads to the points of the soul's origin, which we find to be in the areas of the Pleiades and Sirius.[1]

The original Pyramid was representative of your downward descent into the earth plane from your celestial origins. It also represented a blueprint for uplifting your consciousness. Now you must be able to return to another form, another substance, and this particular device will allow you to re-attune the subtle anatomies to that higher level and dimension of consciousness.

What has transpired is that there have been many souls that have chosen to incarnate in waves from other areas of celestial origin. Now they stand upon the threshold of their capacity to accept themselves as celestial beings, but it has a de-stabilizing effect on their ability to function within society. They become emotionally exhausted in their capacity to stay inspired and to complete their missions and their purposes in the earth plane.

So what your healing does is re-create a capacity for these beings to become more omni-directional. Your healing chamber with light and sound will help to balance them in their capacity to function on the earth plane, and will slowly help them to regain memory of their celestial origins, without becoming disturbed in their function on the earth plane.

Playing the role of the healer allows you to be able to work with the more evolved of these technologies. It allows you to develop the ultimate technology, which, of course, is the human physical form. All things arise out of the needs of the human physical form—the need for healing and various other things. Perhaps you consider yourselves limited, yet as you truly begin to develop these psychic sciences, the whole of your technology, the whole of your society will slowly begin to transform and to serve these technologies. For as these technologies become more practically understood, you will develop the ability to build the appropriate bridges between yourselves and other celestial bodies. There are two standards by which your society is measured. One is your spiritual growth, the other is how evolved your technologies are, and how you would use them in coming into contact with other celestial beings. You have already set a very poor track record, since your more evolved civilizations upon this plane merely sought to subjugate other civilizations by the process of their superior experience in technology.

Ron: An Atlantean civilization, for example?

Atun-Re: Yes, but even as recently as your colonizations with simple inventions such as gunpowder.

That which you have actively involved yourself in is the restoring of a psychic technology that allows for healing on several levels. If you continue to expose yourself to these crystalline structures you will slowly begin to alter your physical form, and to create a greater capacity for self-rejuvenation of the physical body, resulting in less and less need for denser foods, thus ending hunger upon the planet. You would call these things "living simply."

Eventually, you will see that mastering certain elements of fasting and certain elements of insight into healing will reduce the needs of the individual to that which are considered simple living. Simple living will become the very ethics and the very norm of individuals upon this planet. When the individuals reduce their needs, they begin to set up for themselves a whole new moral and ethical pattern. The reason that individuals go to war often deals with issues of what they consider to be limited material resources.

These forms of technology that you build will help individuals to develop a whole new system of ethics and morals by re-aligning the whole of their consciousness. What is considered simple aesthetic spontaneity will become normal, and will eventually become critical to the salvation of one's own consciousness. For instance, you may feel a need to live in a rural environment, because an urban environment has become distracting or disorienting. With this technology, many things that might be considered inappropriate about your civilization will merely begin to fall away. As other individuals begin to subscribe to such devices as these, the whole shape of your civilization will slowly begin to change.

It is not a conquering from without—it is, indeed, a mastering from within, for the individual who masters himself has mastered the world.

Ron: What does meditation lack that this device offers?

Atun-Re: This device merely offers a model. In the past, the ancient priesthood used to go into the temples to provide for themselves a stable space in which to meditate. All this did was create an extremely stable atmosphere in which to quiet the mind.

You have a device that you call a Faraday Cage that screens out all types of different electromagnetic forms, allowing for only the purest of frequency, and therefore the purest of clarity. This particular device does not accomplish meditation, so much as it allows an individual to come into a pure space, and to come totally and wholly into alignment with his or her own personal uniqueness.

Therefore, this device accomplishes the same thing that the ancient temples accomplished. Your healing chamber of sound and light will stabilize the individual's physical form, and this pyramidal device will stabilize their consciousness, but it is up to them to integrate all of these different opportunities that will come to them. It would also be possible for them to eventually accomplish all of their karma with no exposure to any of these devices, but this device speeds and enhances them along their path.

Do you now begin to understand your personal relationship to this device?

Ron: To the device, yes.

Atun-Re: Do you begin to understand your own celestial origins?

Ron: Not enough.

Atun-Re: One moment—I will see if it is for Atun-Re to give any more. The personage known as Deva and the personage known as the Friend, desire to speak of what they call Homeworld. They will speak of these things in what you call "tomorrow's session." What we do reveal, however, is that Deva is your instructor to help you re-align your consciousness, your thoughts and your presence on the earth plane. Deva is primarily a teacher attempting to re-align the planetary grid, whereas, the Friend is the consciousness that bridges that which you call Earth with that which they refer to as Homeworld.

Deva works to coordinate individuals who would build similar devices, to begin to connect the grid to where it may correctly open to absorb the information that, through a form of induction will eventually be communicated through the Friend to the appropriate individuals.

What is transpiring is that you are seeking to become more of a causal being, rather than being emotionally subjective. The emotional framework is needed because of your family unit and the need to communicate with other parties upon this plane. This is why you yourself currently undergo work in the solar plexus area, which is the seat and the source of sensitivity, and of emotional feelings in the earth plane. [I had been feeling tension in my solar plexus area due to absorbing the emotional stresses of others.] We have a question, by what means do you treat yourself in this area?

Ron: None, although the suggestion was given by Deva to use a large silver plaque held over the solar plexus, particularly while treating patients.

Atun-Re: Smart one, this Deva. It helps to project energy that you carry in this area to other persons while healing, and at the same time it also acts as a shield so that you do not pick up their energy. It is an interesting rudimentary reconstruction of what is known as the *Breastplate of Christ*, from the Book of Revelation. It is a device that is used with certain precious stones.

A simple review of the information that we have given: when you have linked the activities of the planetary grid, you will have linked your seven chakras with the seven planetary chakras. When the whole of the planetary grid is linked to the seven planetary chakras, you will then have aligned the planet's own subtle anatomies. This will then create a bridge between your planet and Homeworld.

Ron: Is Homeworld physical, or etheric?

Atun-Re: It is quite physical, although Homeworld's grid is slightly different than your own.

Ron: Does it have seven chakras?

Atun-Re: It actually has twelve chakric systems.

Ron: It is a superior system, then?

Atun-Re: You might put it that way, yes. What will transpire, once connecting appropriate individuals has appropriately linked the planet, there will then ensue an appropriate alignment between your world and Homeworld.

Ron: On the planetary level and on the individual level?

Atun-Re: Yes, both. In the early phases it will be for various individuals. Then, as you begin to link and to reshape the whole of your technology, there will be more direct links with Homeworld, and you will begin to think the thoughts of Homeworld. The thoughts, the achievements and the involvements that are Homeworld's will then become the thoughts and the achievements of your planet. You will then begin to accomplish your original purpose for having chosen to incarnate on this physical plane.

Ron: Myself as an individual?

Atun-Re: For you as an individual, but also as a collective consciousness.

Your device will be inductive in bringing a steady flow of information from Homeworld, which will slowly bring about much of the transformation of the planet in how it perceives itself as a civilization.

You will therefore begin to see individuals that will personify this energy. The result will be that engineers will still think like engineers, and artists will still think like artists, but they will be celestial thinkers.

Do you have questions of Atun-Re?

Ron: None that I would ask at this time. [As interesting as this information was, I was still hoping to hear from Deva and the Friend.]

Deva: I, Deva would come to speak but briefly with you. Indeed there shall be the speaking upon the 'morrow of the issues of that which we would call Homeworld. These shall bring forth the beginning of memories of thy own celestial origins. I, Deva, as known by that name, must now depart from thy midst.

Tom: It has been very pleasant speaking with you, and I do hope we have been of aid. Saints be looking after you. God bless you.

Summary

- Symbolically contained within the structure of the Great Pyramid is the representation of how our planet has come to shape the subtle anatomies, and how we have made sojourns into this plane.

- The Giza Pyramid was not only representative of our downward descent into the earth plane from our celestial origins, but also represented a blueprint for uplifting our consciousness.

- The healing chamber of sound and light will help us regain memory of our celestial origins, without becoming disturbed in our function on the earth plane.

- One of the standards by which a society can be measured is how evolved their technologies are, and how they would use them when coming into contact with other celestial beings.

- Exposure to ethereal technologies will slowly alter our physical form and create a greater capacity for self-regeneration, resulting in less and less need for denser foods.

- When we reduce our needs, we will begin to set up for ourselves a whole new moral and ethical pattern of simple living.

1. A ventilation shaft from the King's Chamber actually points to the region of the sky where the Pleiades and Sirius were apparently situated at the time of the Pyramid's construction.

A Day at the Office

Having just arrived at the office, I once again began preparing for what I can honestly call the true passion of my life. Thinking about another day of healing, I turned on the six-foot waterfall along with some soft background music, uncovered the microscope, and looked at the daily schedule that promised an active day of work.

Never knowing what challenge each person who would walk through the door might offer, I have hardly ever had a chance to develop a routine approach in my practice. Each case has been fascinating and unique, letting me enjoy the process of learning from every patient, endlessly discovering something new.

Once the first patient arrived I switched myself into receiving mode, naturally tuning into them. The alignment of the spine, the assessment of organ function, the determination of energy flows throughout the chakras and acupuncture meridians—all of these are needed to obtain a complete picture of one's state of health. However, intuitive diagnosis is also a state of *becoming* the patient, by stepping into a meditative frame of *no thought* to attain a calm awareness for gaining insight.

The second phase is the treatment. Through study and experience I have acquired various systems for evaluating health, but the treatment itself, for me, is ultimately guided by a natural intuitive response to the patient's *energetic* state. This includes a person's emotional and psychic condition as much as any physical symptom that might have brought them into the office in the first place.

This intuitive approach to healing has gradually become so natural that most of the time I have a sense of being guided by an invisible hand effortlessly and efficiently leading me. In this state of guided awareness not a minute is wasted, no effort goes without some beneficial result, and nothing is done without a feeling of intimate connection with each and every patient.

By the end of the day I normally feel high—the feeling one usually has after running a great race, climbing a lofty peak, or accomplishing a task that, in the deepest part of their being, they always wanted to achieve. For me, experiencing the trust of my patients while responding as best I can to their needs leaves me with a deep feeling of contentment and joy—experiencing life itself through serving others.

12

Homeworld

"It is one of the commonest mistakes to consider that the limit of our power of perception is also the limit of all there is to perceive".

~C.W. Leadbeater

This was the last of four sessions held in two days—the transmissions from Deva and the Friend that answered some of my deepest questions about the order of this universe.

This session was one of the most difficult to comprehend, but it also had the most profound effect I had ever experienced from a channeling. By its end I felt myself a student in the University of the Cosmos, hearing directly from the masters of consciousness.

Atun-Re spoke of going beyond a limited karma-based awareness, developing an ability to receive information and inspiration omni-directionally from various levels and sources of universal spirit. In this awareness, we would move beyond our identity as merely belonging to the earth plane and would begin to think of ourselves as universal beings.

Deva talked about Homeworld, with its many forms of existence, all aware of each other—the quality that we, in our carbon-based physical bodies, are just beginning to develop. As we become acquainted with subtle realities and ethereal beings, this will totally transform our systems of ethics and morals. With such awareness we will then become fully healed in body, mind and spirit, and will create a society of citizens of light.

The Friend made it clear that we here on Earth are not orphaned from the higher planes but simply are in need of reestablishing our awareness of those realms. Many of us have come to Earth as emissaries of spirit to participate in the transformation of consciousness on the planet, and are seeking to establish a natural balance throughout all levels of existence, both within ourselves and in our society. As we accomplish this we will be freed from the weight of karma, which is simply the momentum created by our own past experiences.

*   *   *   *

Ron: I have come to hear from Deva and the Friend.

Tom: Tom McPherson here. How are you doing there?

Ron: Anxious. [Actually, I was feeling enormous anticipation concerning what was about to take place.]

Tom: An honest way of describing it. I do believe that we have some intriguing news. First of all, the instrument [Kevin], in aligning with the energies of Deva and the Friend, may have to undergo a needed adjustment or two. In the meantime, I do believe that Atun-Re would like to communicate a wee bit more concerning some of the issues of Homeworld, as he puts it.

Atun-Re: Atun-Re would come again to speak with you. Do you have a blindfold?

Ron: Yes.

Atun-Re: May we receive this, along with a writing instrument and papyrus, please?

As we have already mentioned, there are the subtle anatomies surrounding your planet. They coordinate with the seven chakras and the seven subtle anatomies that surround you as an individual.

However, now many individuals will begin to take on both the number and function of the subtle anatomies that surround Homeworld. The astral form is that which coordinates known events, and eventually becomes the personality. This will begin to take on an entirely different function, rather than the narrow time flow that you perceive from past lives. You would therefore become more omni-directional, thus taking in information from other diverse solar influences [other solar systems]. The astral body, which usually allows an individual to travel in this plane and still retain the personality, will begin to perceive aspects of other dimensions and lives that have been experienced in other spheres of existence.

Upon incarnation into the earth plane, the astral body is the *veil of forgetfulness* that comes over you and makes you uniquely yourself. The spiritual body is the link with the universal nature, the divine. Together, these would begin to function as one anatomy. You are now beginning to move closer to the twelve subtle anatomies reflective of Homeworld, rather than of the seven subtle anatomies of this particular plane of existence. With the extra functions of these subtle anatomies, you will begin to break out of the identity of merely being part of the physical earth plane, and instead you will begin to think of yourselves as more truly *universal beings*. This awakening of the extra functions of these subtle anatomies will allow an individual to think and to perceive the thoughts of Homeworld.

You are already an individual undergoing such activity. Do you see?

Ron: I do. [He was precisely describing the process that I had felt myself going through over the last two years.]

Atun-Re: This is why it is necessary at times for you to retreat. There is a tendency for you to retreat into the patterns of nature, but do not retreat completely from society itself, otherwise there would be a loss of purpose. For your dharmically remaining links with the earth plane are to bring forth the balance of those things that were rendered in Atlantis, although much of that karma is already fulfilled. You are now becoming a dharmic being, and are helping to bring balance to the appropriate use of some of the planet's technologies. This balance will not only be achieved through technology, as you already sense, but will also be accomplished through the transformation of an individual.

Do you have questions of Atun-Re?

Ron: I have no other questions right now. [I was waiting for Deva and the Friend.]

Atun-Re: Very well.

The Friend, as you say, and Deva, wish for me to communicate a few more things, and then they will speak through.

Homeworld, according to Deva and the Friend, physically exists, but is slightly spatially displaced. You would measure an individual from Homeworld as being more of an ethereal being. In a similar way that this particular earth plane is indeed a multi-racial society, Homeworld has the unusual characteristic of having beings that exist multi-ethereally on different levels and ranges of density.

Ron: Which is also true of the Earth.

Atun-Re: Yes. However, the distinction is that all of the different beings upon Homeworld are fully conscious of each other's existence. Part of your work is to increase an individual's awareness of ethereal reality, which then begins to reshape their spiritual and ethical attitudes. Your intention is to supersede the mundane physical aspects of your patients' realities, and for them to become aware of a greater citizenship and spiritual reality, specifically of an ethereal reality. Your work becomes not so much creating awareness between physical beings and spiritual beings, but becomes more-so creating a *relationship* that is natural between physical beings and ethereal beings. This places the process more in the realm of one's own evolution. The term *spiritual* would then become a new word for what you currently consider to be ethics and morals. Ethics and morals are for individuals who seek to find palatable terms to negotiate limited material resources, whereas, spiritual individuals attempt to be aware of ethereal realities, and this is why, at times, those who tread the spiritual path may appear to be emotionally distant from material reality. Do you see?

Ron: I should. [At times, I had been considered emotionally distant. I had also been longing to actually experience the infinite, not just to hear about it.]

Atun-Re: What we are attempting to give you is a broader vision of Homeworld, and a greater sense of some of the current evolutionary processes that are taking place on this physical plane. We are thus offering you a vision of a current parallel reality of some of your own points of origin, as an "orphan," if you will, from Homeworld. However, the term Homeworld itself should not be considered merely a spatial phenomena, but is a spiritual and ethereal phenomena.

There is also an attempt here to create a sense of purpose, as opposed to a sense of mission, for mission is limited to time schedules. Do you see?

Ron: I'd better see. [I had been feeling pressure to accomplish the construction of the pyramid within a limited time frame, and this was the cause of my growing anxiety.]

Atun-Re: It is more a sense of purpose, for purpose is disconnected from time schedules. Purpose reflects one who is calm within him/herself, and manifests continuously, rather than limiting oneself to a sense of mission.

Some of this body of information is to be shared with other persons. You are like a librarian, a cataloger of this information, thus making it more accessible and coherent. You will eventually be called upon to speak, but only to appropriate parties.

You served one or two lifetimes in that which was known as the Library of Alexandria. You have also experienced long periods of monastic retreat in some of your lifetimes, and it was in these lifetimes upon the earth plane where you were able to gain much of what you consider to be your spiritual awareness. There are currently still periods where you may retreat from the dimensions of physical activity in your daily affairs, for the physical conventions of the earth plane have come to seem alien to you—as alien as an urban environment to someone who has been taken from a natural setting and placed in metropolitan surroundings. Do you see this?

Ron: Yes. [I sometimes wondered where my place on Earth was.]

Atun-Re: For you, these both seem peculiar, because what you attempt to evolve towards is more the ethereal environment, more the spiritual environment. You will find that there will be similar like-minded individuals attracted to you.

We will see what may transpire next with Deva and the Friend. The entity Tom McPherson wishes to return and speak with you very briefly.

Tom: Back again. How are you doing?

Ron: I'm not sure. [Sitting there, I could feel myself being drawn into a vortex of energy and consciousness. I was being lifted out of the realm of rational thought, into a realm of pure ecstatic awareness.]

Tom: Feeling a bit buzzy?

Ron: To say the least.

Tom: A moment here. To put a bit more clearly what Atun-Re was speaking about, there are parallel evolutions going on between what is referred to as Homeworld, and the planet Earth. Your technologies have been taken to such a point that it is possible for the both of you to start making appropriate outreach to each other.

A moment here, I do believe that we have received direct alignment now with Deva. I believe that he will bring through a discourse.

Deva [I accidentally erased the first three minutes of this incredible session, so it begins mid-sentence]:

… unto the quantum of the subatomic, seeking to interrelate unto its higher order of manifestation of the celestial. In Homeworld we have found a stabilization of these forces, and we have created compatibility between physical and ethereal. It is these laws that are sought to be brought to the order of this physical plane. This physical plane's current state of instability is the result of the relationship between, not so much physical beings [as we believe we are], but beings that consist of both the quantum, or physical and biological dimensions of life, or carbon based life-forms, and that which is a higher order of the ethereal.

The biological physical form that you occupy called the physical body is indeed the higher evolved order between the quantum and the ethereal. So thus it is an attempt to stabilize, not so much the physical in relationship to the ethereal, but indeed to stabilize the ethereal in relationship to the quantum: the ability to penetrate into the very heart of the atom, stabilizing the higher ethereal plane in relationship to even that which you consider as sub-atomic.

You consider all thy histories and existences upon this plane as an attempt to stabilize this. This spatially displaces itself as the dynamics that ye consider to be the organizations of ethics and morals, indeed the very force that you consider as civilization—these are but *by-products* of the stabilization of the ethereal to the quantum.

You bring forth devices and concepts of self that seek to bring about a stabilization of these faculties, a stabilization of these forces. The stabilization of these forces is to bring forth an appropriate understanding of the whole of the cosmology, for the cosmology does not mean the extension of the inanimate into the celestial—it means the extension of the celestial wholly into the ultimate animate, which indeed is the quantum. This removes the illusion that, indeed, there is any point of crystallization or measurement along the standards anywhere throughout the cosmology— that there is any point of judgment. For ye are here to reach the final point wherein the individuals would perceive themselves as wholly animate upon all levels of the cosmology.

Upon Homeworld this has been accomplished. The Devic force is the principle that seeks to bring forth the personification of such activities to this plane. In these activities, the next leap in cognizance is that thy plane, which thinks in evolutionary terms and subjects itself to concepts of time and space, must have a new vision of a new concept of its new future.

For without vision, the existences upon this plane, mind ye *existences*, act as an animate force without direction, for ye subject thyselves to spatial concepts of evolution, rather than omni-directional. In this then, ye attach thyselves to measurements of either social standards or even spiritual and visionary standards. Thy ways and thy means must supercede these.

Deva is as the link of consciousness of the planetary force that is personified within each of thee, and the capacity to supercede the personal identity in relationship to this local quantum plane, not physical plane, but quantum plane. For it is foolishness to consider the energies as strictly reduced to the forces of the resistance of the spiritual to the physical. For it is not war upon physical and spiritual, but is indeed more-so harmonics between all levels of the dimensions of the self, and this can only come with the eventual surrender of self, and the giving up of self to total uniqueness.

These then are the forces of Deva. Deva has chosen to anchor self in the expression of that which you call nature, for that is the highest evolution that we have found between all levels of life and all levels of animation, drawing no identity between inanimate and animate, but more-so realizing that consciousness extends to all levels of beings. So thus Deva is the personification of self as linked with the whole of the natural orders and dynamics of this entire plane and order of existence.

We thus then conclude the discourse as to the nature of the force of Deva at this time. There will be a brief pause, and then discourse from the level of the Friend.

Ron: Thank you, Deva.

The Friend:

> *Enoch Kase Sasoth Elohim*
> *Onus Ka Karae Om Elohim*
> *Amanus Um Te Patha Re*
> *Adonaius Elohim Sabaktus*
> *Enum Ounanius Pathau Sai*
> *Kronos Aktum Aunk*
> *Aemanus Elohim Atum Re*

In all of the bodies that you would consider as celestial, we come now into a vibratory presence in the biological dimension so as to give voice to those higher celestial forces. Greetings from the forces that we would come to term Homeworld. Not limited to any spatial form, we find physical focus in the predominant areas of the following: Andromeda, the Pleiades and Sirius, particularly that which is the third solar sun. Greetings from these levels and systems of thought—greetings into the presence of indeed the Elohim. For we find in the higher representative forces other planes of existence. Greetings to those whom have not been as though orphaned by those forces, but to whom there seeks to be the bridge to.

We find the need at times to convey the forces of those existences so that you would, indeed, not lose purpose with that plane; that you would not tire or become weary through separation from the forces that you are, indeed, seeking to manifest upon this plane of existence. For under the activities of the causative forces of this plane you would find thyselves in need of alignment. Ye seek at times to strive to have outreach to the identity of the forces of the Friend and have alignment and identity through same. Know that ye are the natural extensions of the identity of the forces and the faculties that ye term the Friend, for there seeks to be through that name, as it is subjectively used in the earth plane, a bridge between thyselves and the forces that are indeed Homeworld.

We find, indeed, that these are not to shape thy consciousness so much as to uplift it. It is indeed thy purpose and thy expression to become somewhat the orders and the forces of this plane—not to seek governance over the subjective forces that also seek to link their presence here, but more-so to uplift them and make them knowledgeable of the existence of the higher forces.

You have brought forth knowledge, technologies, and sciences as uplifted from the Friend, but also you would find that they not only come subjectively from the source of the Friend, but are indeed raised to the level of thy own vibration and thy capacity to remember the forces from thy days and thy incarnations upon Homeworld.

Even though you come here, ye link thyselves karmicly with the plane not through direct action, but more so by setting forth technologies for the actions, that you would be allowed to reside here as a historical activity in this plane. As a historical activity you bring about a shift in both consciousness and subtle social forces, strictly by the context of thy own presence and systems of thought. Ye are, indeed, to bring inspiration by editing those systems of thought, even if you are not to directly contribute by the spoken presence. For these are, as though, the lesser forces.

Ye are not to lobby amidst those who have chosen physical citizenry here, but indeed you are more so to slowly bring about the alteration as a growing presence. Eventually it is sensed that it is not measured by the success of multitudes but by the growing presence of the very forces, altering the concept of space-time as it is considered here, to bring about measurable results of a new system, a new thought and technology. For ultimately the human instrumentality in the biological dimension that you call life and humanity itself, will become that technology in its own right.

Ye have been taught in even the most ancient of the evolved civilizations that the experience of this subjective plane has been brought into focus, through that which you call Lemuria and Atlantis. We seek not to restore the technologies of the past, but to bring forth appropriate perception of the ability of the evolvement of consciousness upon this plane. So thus the bridge with Homeworld.

Homeworld is, indeed, a spatial phenomenon, existing straddling seven different dimensions. It is, indeed, a physical existence to those who perceive upon the carbon based life forms. It is more so an ethereal pattern even as you would seek to bring its forces into influence. It is, indeed, a radiant place of light, coordinating most of its technologies through massive crystalline presences of stabilized silicon, stabilized carbon, stabilized titanium, carbon forms, and various other materials that you would consider, as though, shining and iridescent in their existence and their beauty upon this plane. For the attraction to these forms has never been to those upon a truly ethereal and spiritual dimension, but more so the wealth that they would gather in material resources.

For indeed the material is not even a lesser dimension. It is to be passed through, even as one would pass through the atmospheres, simply to draw the essence of thy being from these planes, but not to lose thy oneness with the higher celestial dimensions.

The subjectivity that ye have chosen to express in these physical carbon-based life forms is that you are indeed choosing to manifest these as one more crystalline form. For look upon them in their various states and you would find that they are based upon various crystal technologies that ye seek to stabilize upon the appropriate ethereal levels, the by-product of which is, indeed, physical harmony, which ye would call the science of healing.

Ye adapt it to the subjective needs of this plane, but indeed it is more so a higher force, a higher level of existence. So therefore ye slowly begin to bring forth the unifying thought that indeed is Homeworld, and that is a natural harmonics between all the levels of the higher dimensions. Indeed, ye are emissaries of that thought, and indeed *are* that thought, both one and the same.

Thy subjective experiences are but the coordination of the harmonics in the physical plane. For indeed, even by thy presence, ye alter. Even by thy presence, ye become as those laws. Even by thy presence, ye anchor the purpose and the structure of Homeworld upon this plane.

For Homeworld is not a superior spatial point as though to have focus. It is but one point in an ongoing process of the whole that, indeed, you would term the physical universe, and indeed, all would eventually become as uplifted. For ultimately ye are the evolutionary force in each purpose and expression that you would manifest and bring forth. All the levels of personality that you seek to focus upon are but the vocabulary of that ultimate expression, not through the surrender of the personality, but the discovery of uniqueness.

Here then, the Friend as the bridge with the spatial phenomenon that you call Homeworld must, not depart, but become more the presence of through thy own presence, as you would perceive and, indeed, even accept as an active force. Take then the subjective words that we are able to impress through this carbon expression, this carbon crystallization that you call an instrumentality or medium-ship, but never surrender your uniqueness. Always become, indeed, as the law, rather than under it, and know that it has always been in same.

The Friend now would as depart, but say as Enoch,

> *Elasot Emonum Adonai*
> *Carbvitol Enunum Atum Sumptum*
> *Cintuse Atum Mus*
> *Alum Elohim Akum Adonai*

Tom: Back again. A moment here, while I adjust the carbon-based life form. How are you doing there?

Ron: Incredible. [I was aware that the light of the divine was shining on me and within me, and I was losing all sense of a separate self. The feeling of love and grace was more than I could hold as I felt myself drawn into a wonderful state of joy and peace.]

How are *you* doing, Tom?

Tom: Very good. Well, I will tell you what—we wish to leave you most singularly with this moment, and so we will withdraw rather quickly.

Most pleasant speaking with you. Saints be looking after you. God bless you.

John: Hail. Seek to be at peace which those things that you receive from spirit, for we find that they are the fruit of thy Father's works, and indeed, ye are that work. Welcome to thy Father's Light. God bless you. Amen.

Summary

- By expanding the functions of our subtle anatomies, we will begin to break out of our identity as merely being part of the physical earth plane, and will start to think of ourselves as truly universal beings.

- Increasing our awareness of ethereal reality will begin to reshape our spiritual and ethical attitudes.

- Our technologies have been taken to such a point that it is possible for both our planet and what is referred to as Homeworld to start making appropriate outreach to each other.

- We must now expand beyond our linear concepts of evolution, in which we limit ourselves by either social or visionary standards, and begin to perceive omni-directionally.

- From the standpoint of spirit there is no separation between animate and inanimate, because consciousness extends to all levels of creation.

- The purpose of contact with beings such as Deva and the Friend is not to shape our consciousness with ideas and beliefs, but to raise our own awareness that we ourselves are beings of energy and light.

- The material world is not a lesser dimension, and is to be passed through, but without losing our oneness with the higher celestial dimensions.

- The physical carbon-based life forms called the physical body are themselves based upon various crystalline technologies, which we seek to stabilize upon the appropriate ethereal levels.

- Homeworld is not a superior location in the cosmos, but is one point in an ongoing process of expansion of consciousness in what we call the physical universe.

Part Two

Healing
In the
Future

The following two chapters were inspired by channelings in which John, one of my spirit guides, spoke on the future of healing and the nature of intuition. The channeled information is mainly presented in its original form, some statements being correlated to the modern scientific research.

The Path to Regeneration

The future of the healing arts lies in bringing full awareness to the mind, body and spirit, thus aligning an individual with the divine, whereby the body may attain the ability of complete regeneration.

As the mind awakens to a greater awareness, the cell structures of the body begin to vibrate more closely to the rate of the spiritual self. This awakening allows the qualities of one's own spirit to be carried throughout the body via the psychic energy channels found within the energetic anatomy. These channels carry the life force throughout the physical form, emerging as points in the acupuncture meridians. The process of energy movement and transfer can be compared to the circulatory system, which transports oxygen taken in through the lungs to every organ and cell of the body.

The practice of the physician, therefore, will be similar to the practice of yoga, bringing about the union of the body, mind and spirit through the neuro-meridian pathways, which are the sum total of the neurological system, located in the physical anatomy, and the meridian system, found in the energetic anatomy.

Our health can be affected in many ways. A weakening of the vital energy of the Earth, a reduction of the physical nutrients available to the body, contamination of the environment, the experience of harmful psychic states—all these disrupt the flow of the life force, leading to disturbances in the physical body and thus a shortened lifespan.

Therefore, healing in the future will involve the channeling of the life force to all portions of the anatomy. This will include creating an unrestricted flow of vitality into the cellular tissues as well as into the molecular and sub-atomic levels that form them.

In the Eastern systems of thought there are three primary blockages to the flow of the life force. These are located in the chakras, or energy wheels, of the subtle anatomy. These three "knots" are found in the base chakra at the coccyx, the heart chakra in the chest, and the crown chakra at the top of the head. In the process of total regeneration, these centers will become activated, releasing the kundalini, or vital force.

Directing one's awareness within, to the self, will be one of the essential ingredients for this awakening. This process will be supported by individual techniques of prayer and meditation, control of the breath, pure diet, and even such seemingly unrelated factors as evaluation of one's work and relationships—all of which will ultimately promote the awakening of *cellular consciousness*[1].

This will naturally result in the divination of the physical body, facilitating the alignment of the various dimensional aspects of an individual with what may be called their *divine blueprint*.

Through the development of a system of total healing, the entire body will come into a single pitch or tone. Each portion of the body will be brought into harmony with every other part. This process might be compared to a symphony, where various instruments are played simultaneously, and yet all are tuned to one precise tone before the beginning of a concert, so that they may sound in harmony.

The God-enlightened physical form may allow for the complete and total function of the neuro-meridians. The stem cells would then continuously flow throughout the body, which might lead to an ongoing renewal of the physical form itself. This process would conceivably result in life spans that could be greatly extended. Some have called this the *Methuselah effect*.[2]

The process of increasing the levels of living energy flowing along the neuro-meridian pathways may be the single-most important factor in activating the stem cells throughout the body. Some of these cells have the capacity to develop into almost any cell, potentially bringing about healing and regeneration of any portion of the physical anatomy. Through the combined effects of various forms of natural healing, the stem cells might be encouraged to migrate from the abdomen, bone marrow and elsewhere, bringing about tissue repair to the affected areas. This process of stem cell activation might conceivably lead to a total regeneration of the entire physical form.

It has also been medically observed that in areas of injury, where tissue regeneration begins to occur, there can be a movement of stem cells and *de-differentiated cells* to other unrelated areas of injury for the formation of *blastema*. This process can sometimes bring about a healing of scar tissue, and might occasionally even lead to the repair of damaged internal organs, actually producing the remission of disease. This phenomenon of tissue regeneration is not unknown within the current field of medicine.[3]

The practice of the holistic practitioner supports the body, mind and spirit through the use of acupuncture, chiropractic, homeopathy, herbs, supplements and other natural healing methods to bring an individual into a greater alignment. In addition, there have always been healing systems for manipulating the subtle energies surrounding the physical body, based on conducting the flow of life force through the healer's hands. The future physician may also come to perceive the energy field in a way that might be described as "clairvoyant" or "clear seeing." This faculty would further aid in a healer's ability to affect changes in the subtle anatomies, and to awaken the body's dormant capacity for regeneration, made latent due to a lack of flow of the life force.

1. According to Dr. Lipton, author of *The Biology of Belief,* the cell membrane is an organic form of a computer chip, the cell's equivalent of a brain. His research shows that the environment, operating through the membrane, controls the behavior and physiology of the cell and is able to turn the genes on and off. His discoveries go against the established scientific opinion that physiology is ultimately controlled by genes, and define the molecular pathways connecting the mind with the body.

2. Methuselah is the oldest person mentioned in the book of Genesis, who was said to have died at the age of nine hundred and sixty nine.

3. Dean Ornish, MD and Robert Becker, MD have already demonstrated the body's capacity for regeneration of tissues that were previously thought unable to repair themselves except for minor ways.

Intuition & Science

The marriage of intuition and science, which might also be called the union of *intuition* and *reason*, encourages the development of a practitioner's own intuitive awareness, which will be the key element in healing in the future.

Full consciousness is the phenomena of direct knowing, requiring all portions of the brain to perform synergistically together. In the study of the nervous system, it is currently recognized that certain functions of the brain typically remain compartmentalized, or isolated, from each other. Therefore, to achieve full brain capacity there must be a synchronization of the brain areas, leading to a state of total awareness and comprehension. Such physical integration of the brain's hemispheres occurs via structures such as the *corpus callosum*, consisting of billions of nerve cells that physically connect the two sides of the brain, and thus correlate different aspects of the personality. What is more, this physical unification of the brain parallels the energetic integration of one's subtle anatomies.

Awareness then becomes the link between the neurological system and the meridian system. Together, these are known as the neuro-meridian system, and as long as an individual exists within a physical body, their awareness primarily functions on the level of the neuro-meridians.

The ability to translate the vibratory quality of the life force, consciously, into the meridians, and then into the physical neurological system, or brain, ultimately manifests as an ability to experience energy fields through pure awareness. This ability then produces a conscious perception of the life force on all levels of existence.

As already demonstrated by science, the body's physiological functions are ultimately molecular in nature, and all molecular dynamics are also energetic. This is the foundation, for instance, of homeopathy, Bach Flowers and *water memory*[1]. Therefore, the key to recognizing the dysfunctional patterns in the energetic and physical anatomies is in perceiving the patterns of balance and imbalance upon the molecular level itself. Interestingly, this is also the means to their restoration.

Healing therefore involves the return of a healthy energetic pattern initially from the electromagnetic to the molecular, then from the molecular to the electrochemical, from the electrochemical to the physiological, from the physiological to the metabolic, and finally from the metabolic to full cellular function and memory, thus reaching the denser anatomical levels. It is at this last level of cellular function that the success or failure of healing is often measured by allopathic medicine. On the other hand, holistic medicine might measure its success by the ability to identify and correct the original cause of disease by re-establishing balance at the electromagnetic stage of the disturbance.

Only when there is the full integration of the brain-mind complex, and a complete and balanced flow of energy throughout the neuro-meridian system, is there then a wave of consciousness that flows between the resultant balanced hemispheres of the brain. This, in turn, produces a stimulation of the pituitary and pineal glands, the *liquid crystal*[2] centers in the brain where awareness becomes fully developed and experienced. Ultimately, these crystal centers are the actual seats of the ability to be conscious of molecular states, and thus to be fully aware of the life force as it exists on all levels of creation.

Therefore, with improved neurological function there is a shift from using only the left or right hemisphere of the brain to the enhanced integration of one's physical and energetic anatomies. This shift then has the potential to produce a result that becomes far more than just the sum total of isolated parts. Indeed, it may actually allow for a gradual increase in conscious awareness of the divine, even while still remaining in the physical body.

It is interesting that in this process of utilizing one's conscious awareness, many people may bypass the initial analytical phase because of the subliminal, or subconscious nature of their knowledge. They may therefore go directly into the awareness-intuitive-analytical cycle, which is called *clairvoyance*. The key element here, which is often misunderstood, is in the function of pure awareness, which is the capacity of an individual to be aware throughout their entire energy field, and thus to perceive the various levels of creation via their own field's omnipresent and unlimited capacity for consciousness.[3]

The issue of consciousness translates into the merger of the analytical with the intuitive, which may then lead to pure awareness. With an increase in consciousness there is an increased tendency to benefit the whole, whereas with a reduction in consciousness there is a tendency to benefit only a portion. Perhaps this is why, with an elevated consciousness, there may be more compassion for others, since through awareness we gain empathy. This offers profound implications for the social, political and economic choices we make on a planet-wide scale, as our growing awareness increasingly reflects our concern for the whole.

The traditional concept of distinguishing between intuition and reason merely arises from the old paradigm that the intuitive functions have not yet become integrated with the analytical faculties, thus resulting in a split between the intuitive and the rational. However, this limitation is actually a by-product of the *critical*, or *deconstructive* processes of the mind, not the *analytical* ones. In fact, the intuitive capacities of the mind-brain function may actually lie in the ability to remove the restrictions of the critical, or *deconstructive* aspects of the mind, and to then utilize the mind's inherent capacity for *holism*. Holism is the practice of holding all aspects of an inquiry in inter-relationship with each other, which then naturally brings the faculty of intuition into the process. It is the critical faculty itself that blocks the intuition, whereas it is consciousness that nurtures it. Similarly, self-critical qualities tend to limit an individual, whereas self-analytical ones lead towards self-advancement. [Judging versus understanding or discernment.]

Science is currently trying to understand the subconscious processes natural to the mind's function. As it applies to the practice of healing, the state of an intuitive healer's awareness can be described as *mindfulness*, or the capacity for *pure awareness*, which is then integrated with the ability for practical analysis.

Let us take a look at how this level of increased awareness might be achieved. First of all, in the field of consciousness, pure awareness is non-judgmental, and is linked to the intuitive state. Therefore, the healer's elevated consciousness is an essential part in the health evaluation process. Following conscious perception, there is then the correlating of the rational with the intuitive, which permits each hemisphere of the brain to make its contribution to the practitioner's awareness.

Through pure awareness, the healer directly senses the various energetic functions taking place within the patient, knowing that these energetic properties are the true undercurrents for all measurable aspects of physiology.

An example of this integrative approach might be a health practitioner's ability to see the relationship between a patient's abdominal pain and a hidden anxiety pattern, possibly originating from career or financial concerns. This emotional conflict might create a disturbance in the solar plexus, the region corresponding to one's sense of personal power and self-esteem, thus adversely affecting physiological functions of the stomach.

The practitioner might then not only utilize various healing techniques to treat physical aspects of the disturbance, but could also employ counseling to aid a patient in achieving a higher level of emotional and mental clarity. Whereas the use of medication might merely have provided some relief from physical discomfort, the patient's needs could only be fully met by helping them to overcome psychological issues, resulting in an improved energetic balance in the area of concern.

Therefore, the union of intuition and science, when viewed from the perspective of health care, leads to the healer's ability to reestablish a patient's balance and harmony on both physical and non-physical levels of existence. In other words, the physician aids in restoring a whole person through inter-cooperation with that person's own innate capability for regeneration.

1.   Masaru Emoto's work, presented in his book *The Hidden Messages in Water,* provides us with factual evidence that human vibrational energy, thoughts, words, ideas and music all affect the molecular structure of water, the very same water that comprises over seventy percent of a human body and covers the same amount of our planet.

2.   Liquid crystal is a phase of matter having a form between a liquid and a crystal.

3.   In 1946, Paramahansa Yogananda published *Autobiography of a Yogi*, in which he described his first experience of cosmic awareness—the ability to become aware throughout one's entire energy field.

Part Three

The Great Pyramid

Mysteries of the Great Pyramid

> "The Pyramid was built both as an initiation chamber for consciousness, and as a time capsule, to 'monumentalize the science of the time for another civilization far in the future.'"
>
> ~Peter Tomkins
> *Secrets of the Great Pyramid*

According to common astrological knowledge, mankind develops in 2160-year cycles, which are major periods of human experience defined by celestial influence. Soon, we would eventually complete the Age of Pisces, also known as the *age of belief*, and would enter into the Age of Aquarius, called the *age of knowledge*. One Great Year, consisting of twelve of these Ages, would take nearly 26,000 years to complete. Although this monumental cycle of Earth's wobble, or precession, was once thought to be the discovery of the Greek astronomer Hipparchus, who lived about 2,000 B.C.E. [*Before the Common Era*], there is evidence in ancient astronomical maps that this knowledge actually dates much further back, as far as at least 4,000 B.C.E.

Many indigenous cultures unaware of modern scientific discoveries preserve legends of lost continents and vanished civilizations, which, most likely, have been passed down verbally from one generation to another. In recorded history, Plato and several other Greek and Roman authors also brought up the myth of Atlantis as an ancient race wiped out by cataclysmic changes on Earth. Presumably, Plato heard of Atlantis from a Greek statesman who, in turn, had received the story of the lost continent from the Egyptians.

Interestingly, although the contemporary world looks at the Greeks as the originators of modern arts and sciences, many of them, including Sophocles, Solon, Cicero, Pindar, Herodotus, Dioclosus, and even the famed Pythagoras and Plato, all stated that they were initiates of Egypt. Pythagoras himself, often known as the father of Greek mathematics, lived as a priest in Egypt for over twenty years, as did Plato for several years as well. Indeed, the knowledge they gained in the Middle East later became the foundation for much of their wisdom. In fact, the five-pointed star that was the secret symbol of recognition for the Pythagoreans had its lines intersecting with each other in the exact proportion of the *Golden Mean,* one of the fundamental principles in the Great Pyramid construction!

Back in ancient days, astronomical knowledge not only pertained to the physical aspects of star configurations, but was also integrated into astrology as a means for understanding the great cycles of human evolution. The Great Pyramid itself was apparently built on sacred principals known only to a small group of aspirants for the purpose of initiating them into life's mysteries.

Of the three pyramids of the Giza complex, the Great Pyramid is the tallest, and is the only one to have sides angled precisely at 51 degrees, 50 minutes, thus forming the *Pi* and *Phi* relationship. The bases of all three pyramids are precisely aligned to the cardinal points of the compass and form a diagonal line running from northeast to southwest. Even more intriguing is the theory that the pattern of the three pyramids may also represent the three stars of the Belt of Orion in the constellation of the Hunter, located between the Pleiades and Sirius. If we project the angle of the three pyramids back in time, they precisely align with Orion's Belt in the year 10,450 B.C.E., the period when many now believe the Great Pyramid may have been constructed.[1]

The Pyramid was built on top of a huge, underground mountain of granite bedrock, able to support the weight of the colossal stone structure throughout the ages. Its surface was covered in limestone, which has a quality of becoming more polished and reflective as it is exposed to weather and abrasive desert sands. Exceeding 450 feet, or as high as a 48-story building, the Pyramid's surface would reflect the sun so brightly that it could be visible from the Moon. Observed by Herodotus about four hundred years B.C.E, it was described as "highly polished in limestone blocks in which one could scarcely even see the joints between them."

The history of the first modern age explorations of the Great Pyramid goes back to the year 820 C.E. [*the Common Era*] and belongs to the Arab prince Abdullah Al Mamun, known for patronizing the arts and sciences, and translating some of the works of the famous Greek mathematician and astronomer Ptolemy into the Arabic language.

Al Mamun claimed that the inspiration to explore the Great Pyramid came about through a dream, in which the famous Greek philosopher, Aristotle, requested that he develop a map of the heavens. Through his own sources Al Mamun was informed that along with other treasures, the Pyramid contained a secret chamber with maps of the celestial sphere, and this inspired his decision to find a way into its depths.

Having gathered a group of engineers and architects, the prince commissioned them to find a way into the Pyramid. Unfortunately, in their intense search of the steep polished surface of the massive stony structure, they were unable to discover any clues to a doorway. Unaccustomed to giving up, Al Mamun decided to tunnel manually through the solid limestone, but hammer and chisel, the tools of the time, were too slow, and obviously not up to the task.

In frustration, he eventually chose a completely different method. A large fire was built directly against the stony sides of the Pyramid, and then vinegar was thrown onto the hot rocky surface, causing it to fragment. The cracked stone was rammed, broken loose, and carried away.

In this way the prince and his men tunneled through one hundred feet of solid rock into the core of the Pyramid, but still did not find anything up to their expectations. Just when Al Mamun had finally resigned himself to failure, his workers broke through into one of the shafts, now known as the Descending Passage. This passage led them to what later became known as the Pit, then to the Queen's Chamber, and eventually to the King's Chamber above. There, inside the King's Chamber, they discovered a large stone sarcophagus—a coffin-like structure typically used for storing a mummified body normally belonging to royalty.

Many modern historians have believed that the Great Pyramid was the burial site of King Khufu, an ancient Egyptian ruler, also known under his Greek name of Cheops. Apparently, this may not have been the case, for when Al Mamun's men entered the Pyramid they discovered that the lidless sarcophagus in the King's Chamber was totally empty! In fact, there was no sign of any kind of mummy buried there and only a few bits of wood and stone were ever found inside. Apparently, the Great Pyramid had never been constructed for use as a tomb, as many had previously thought, but had been designed for an entirely different purpose.

Besides finding no treasure, the Arab prince apparently was also never able to decipher any of the secrets of astronomy and proportion disguised in the Pyramid's massive structure, which must have been a profoundly frustrating experience.

The Pyramid was to maintain its secrets of astronomical and esoteric knowledge, so diligently sought by Al Mamun, for another 800 years. In 1638, British mathematician and astronomer John Greaves embarked upon a mission to Egypt, where he hoped to find clues to the Earth's dimensions in the design of the Great Pyramid.

Greaves, who painstakingly explored and measured the structure, can be credited with re-discovering that the Pyramid is both a mandala that embodies the secrets of creation and the key for unlocking those secrets.

More than one world conqueror has visited the Pyramid. After Napoleon Bonaparte had swept through Egypt, he decided to spend some time in solitude in the King's Chamber, just as Alexander the Great presumably did before him. On coming out, the general appeared pale and shaken, and when asked if he had experienced anything unusual, categorically refused to discuss the matter. After becoming emperor many years later, Napoleon still declined to speak of the incident, although hinting that he had received some form of insight into his destiny. Later in life, having bordered on confiding in a friend, he was described as shaking his head, saying: "No. What's the use? You'd never believe me."[2]

Throughout its long and tumultuous history, the Great Pyramid has always been thought of as a wonder, because of its enigmatic properties and the mysteries related to its architecture and design.

The height of the structure equals 146.52 meters, the base 230.36 meters on a single side, and the *apothem* [the distance from the highest point, or apex, of the Pyramid to the middle of the base of one side] 186.37 meters.

If we take the entire circumference of the Pyramid and divide it by twice its height, we will come up with Pi, or 3.1415, the ratio of the diameter of a circle to its circumference [(4 X 230.36)/(2 X 146.52) = 3.14].

If we take the apothem of the Pyramid, and divide it by half the length of a side, we will come up with Phi, or 1.618, known as the *Golden Ratio, Golden Mean* or *Golden Proportion* [186.37/(230.36/2) = 1.618]. [3]

A pyramid designed with the exact proportions of Pi and Phi incorporates the two most universal principals found in nature and in mathematics. The pyramid could be large or small, but the proportions remain the same.[4]

These proportions were chosen because they are instrumental in the creation of a structure that is in resonance with the universal principals of energy movement and creation in matter. In fact, the Pyramid is a huge, finely tuned resonator. Like a radio that can be tuned-in to a broadcasting station, the Pyramid was dialed-in to the resonant frequency of the Earth, as well as to certain locations and frequencies found in space.

The Pyramid was also attuned to the molecules of quartz crystal, and even to the water molecule itself. The angle of the inter-crystalline lattice that makes up quartz crystal is 52 degrees, which is also the angle of one side of a pyramid when it is built to the exact proportions of Pi and Phi. Perhaps even more fascinating, doubling this number will result in 104 degrees, which is, by no coincidence, the angle between the molecular bonds of water, composed of hydrogen and oxygen in the form of H_2O. Thus, the molecular structure of water, which comprises about two thirds of the human body, not only matches the configuration of a quartz crystal, but is also reflected in the design of the Great Pyramid. This harmonic allows for transference of the energy of the Pyramid into the physical body through the principle of resonance.

As mentioned earlier, dividing the perimeter of the Great Pyramid by twice its height results in 3.14, or Pi, the value famous for determining the circumference of a circle from its radius. This means that the height of the Pyramid corresponds to the radius of a circle, and the circumference of its base correlates to the perimeter of a sphere. This is an astounding finding! This proportion actually allows the straight-sided structure of the Pyramid to correspond to the round shaped structure of a sphere. Some researchers even believe that the dimensions of the perimeter of the Pyramid may represent the circumference of the Earth, where its apex corresponds to the North Pole. Other mathematical mysteries, such as the distance of the Earth to the Sun, may also be reflected in the construction of the Pyramid.

The magical proportions of both Pi and Phi, which were the foundational principals in building the Pyramid, are also found throughout nature, as in the proportion of the width of a leaf to its length, in the placement of the wings of a bird in relation to the length of its body, or in the proportions of the outward flowing spirals of a seashell. Perhaps the most well known proponent of the Golden Mean was the Renaissance artist, scientist and inventor Leonardo Da Vinci, whose timeless masterpieces reflect the harmony of creation.

It is believed that Plato himself referred to the Golden Ratio as one of the universal mathematical building blocks. Could it be just a coincidence that the Great Pyramid is almost perfectly oriented to the North, although the magnetic compass was invented only five hundred years ago; that its form incorporates the functions of both Pi and the Golden Mean; and that the King's Chamber itself incorporates the precise proportions of 3-4-5 in the dimensions of its floor plan? The 3-4-5 ratio made its discoverer, Pythagoras, famous and is known as the foundation of modern mathematics, which translates as $a^2 + b^2 = c^2$, or 3X3(or 9) + 4X4(or 16) = 5X5(or 25).

Another interesting fact is that Leonardo Fibonacci, a distinguished Italian mathematician, created another link between the ancient and modern worlds of knowledge by introducing the method of deriving the value of Phi through a series of simple mathematical calculations.

During the turn of the 12th to 13th centuries C.E., Fibonacci, the son of an Italian diplomat, traveled to the Middle East, where he encountered what had been preserved of the Ancient Egyptian mathematical school. There, he learned the simpler, more elegant Hindu numeric system, based on the numerals 1 through 9. Fibonacci's introduction of this new system of notation to Europe constituted liberation from the unwieldy Roman numerals in use up to that time. As already mentioned, Fibonacci also brought the additive series based on Phi,[5] which came to bear his name, and which served as a vehicle for bringing awareness of the Golden Section to the great minds and artists of Europe.

Interestingly, the *reciprocal* of Phi, found by dividing it into 1, is 0.618 [1/1.618 = 0.618]. This number is very close to the number 0.666, which is 2/3.

By dividing the whole into one third and two-thirds, we arrive at the *law of thirds*, known through its use by photographers and artists for creating a feel of balance and proportion in their work.

There are many remaining mysteries about the Great Pyramid, as well as about those who erected it. May the universal knowledge now being revealed serve mankind on its path to a more conscious existence on Earth.

1. Some modern researchers believe that, based on studies of the wear patterns from wind and rain on the Sphinx, both the Great Pyramid and the Sphinx were originally constructed six to twelve thousand years ago—much older than was originally believed.

2. Described by Peter Tompkins in his book *Secrets of the Great Pyramid.*

3. Gyorgy Doczi has written a fully illustrated book on the Golden Proportion under the title *The Power of Limits—Proportional Harmonies in Nature, Art and Architecture.*

4. The pyramidal device described in this book was also built to the exact proportions of Pi and Phi.

5. The *Fibonacci Series* is derived in a very interesting way. Begin with the numbers 1 and 2. Divide 2 by 1 and you get 2. Add 1 and 2 together to get 3, then divide 3 by the last number you added, (2), to get 1.5. Add 3 to the number you just divided by, (2), and you get 5, then divide by the last number, (3), and you get 1.66. Continue in this manner, and within ten of these cycles you arrive at 1.618, which is Phi. Phi [the Golden Mean], like Pi [the ratio of the diameter of a circle to its circumference], will never be an exact number, and you may work out as many numbers following the decimal point, as you are willing to calculate. The further you continue the series, the more precise the calculations will be.

Photos and Sketches

The Pleiades
Photo by Chuck Vaughn

The top of the pyramid
With the capstone removed

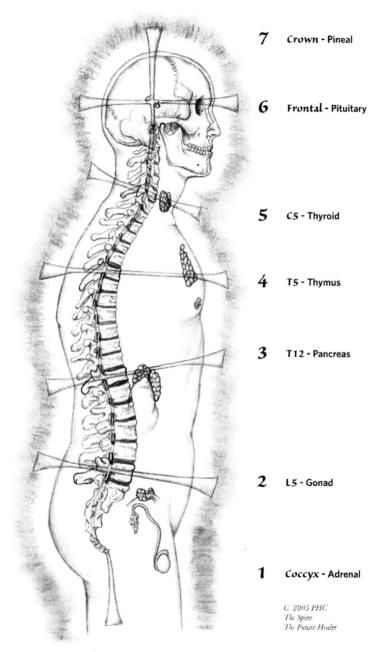

7   **Crown - Pineal**

6   **Frontal - Pituitary**

5   **C5 - Thyroid**

4   **T5 - Thymus**

3   **T12 - Pancreas**

2   **L5 - Gonad**

1   **Coccyx - Adrenal**

C 2005 PHC
The Spine
The Future Healer

The glands and vertebrae
Corresponding to the chakras

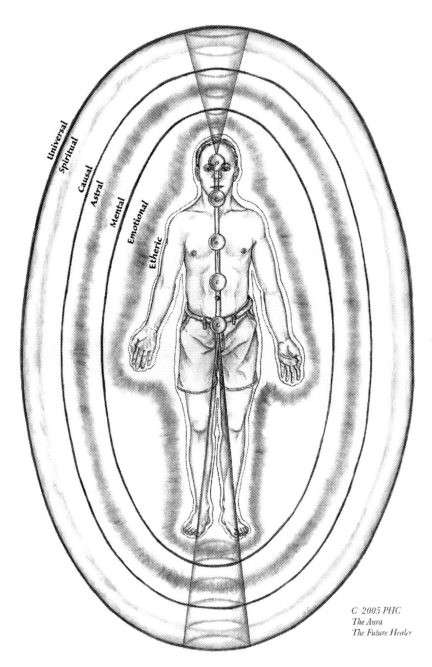

Universal
Spiritual
Causal
Astral
Mental
Emotional
Etheric

C 2005 PHC
The Aura
The Future Healer

The seven layers of the aura

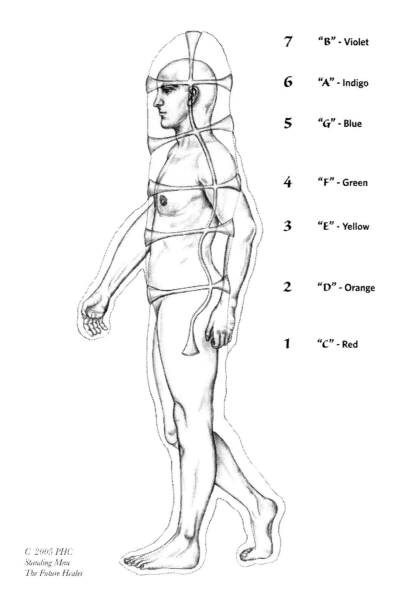

7 "B" - Violet

6 "A" - Indigo

5 "G" - Blue

4 "F" - Green

3 "E" - Yellow

2 "D" - Orange

1 "C" - Red

C 2005 PHC
Standing Man
The Future Healer

The colors and musical tones
Corresponding to the chakras

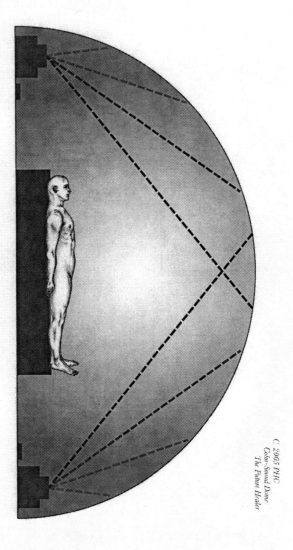

Color Sound Dome

C 2005 PHC
Color-Sound Dome
The Future Healer

The aspirant, immersed in vibration,
Sound and light

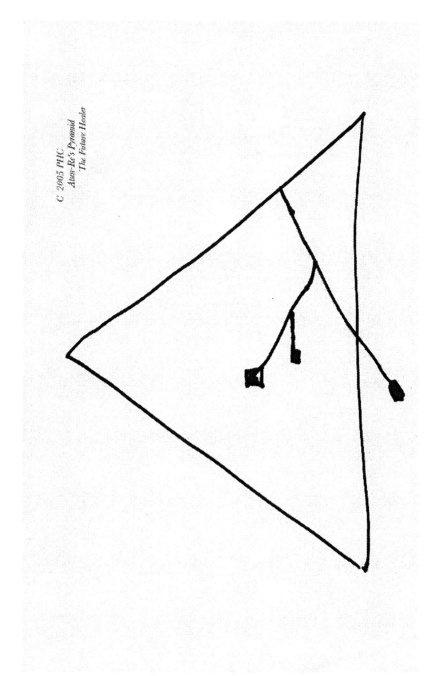

Atun-Re's blindfolded drawing of the pyramid

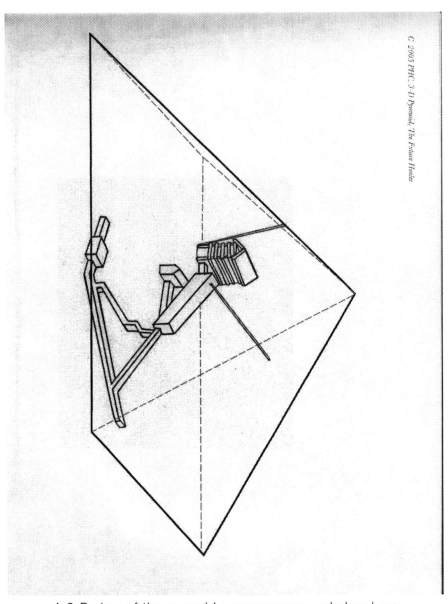

A 3-D view of the pyramid passageways and chambers

Inside the Great Pyramid

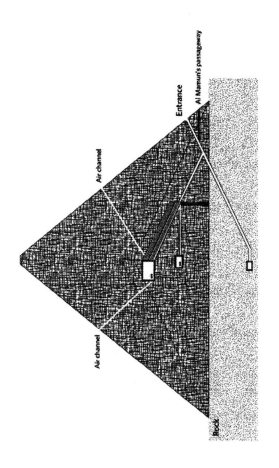

The Great Pyramid—the only one
Known to have air channels.
The King's Chamber lies at the Phi point

The pyramidal device

Relation of a Hemisphere to a Π Pyramid

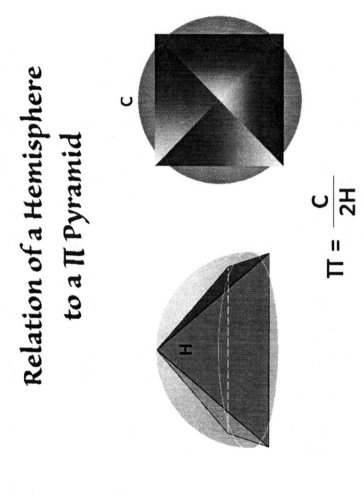

$$\Pi = \frac{C}{2H}$$

In a Π pyramid, the perimeter of the base equals the circumference of the sphere

© 2005 PHC
Pi Pyramid
The Future Healer

A Pi Pyramid, whose height and circumference
Equal that of a hemisphere

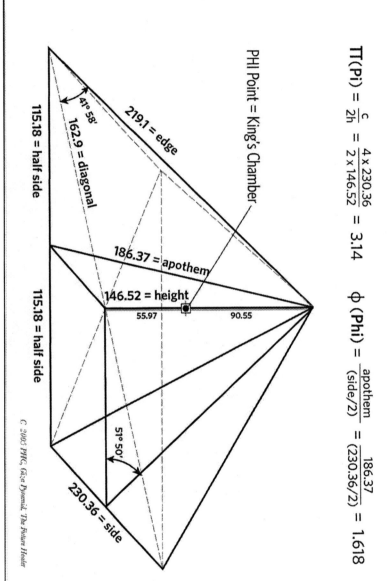

Giza Pyramid

$$\pi (\text{Pi}) = \frac{c}{2h} = \frac{4 \times 230.36}{2 \times 146.52} = 3.14$$

$$\phi (\text{Phi}) = \frac{\text{apothem}}{(\text{side}/2)} = \frac{186.37}{(230.36/2)} = 1.618$$

PHI Point = King's Chamber

41° 58'

162.9 = diagonal

219.1 = edge

115.18 = half side

186.37 = apothem

146.52 = height

55.97   90.55

115.18 = half side

51° 50'

230.36 = side

© 2005 PHC, Giza Pyramid, The Future Healer

The dimensions of the Great Pyramid

PHI = Pythagorus Secret Code

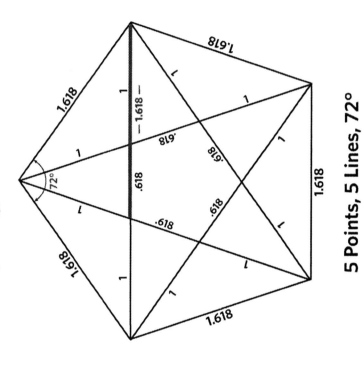

5 Points, 5 Lines, 72°

Each line of the pentagram is in a
Golden Proportion to the whole

The Giza complex of three pyramids,
Which aligned with the three stars in the Belt of Orion around 10,450
B.C.E.—The time when the Great Pyramid may have been built.

$$1 \quad \frac{2}{1} \quad \frac{3}{2} \quad \frac{5}{3} \quad \frac{8}{5}$$

$$(2.0) \quad (1.5) \quad (1.666) \quad (1.6)$$

$$\frac{13}{8} \quad \frac{21}{13} \quad \frac{34}{21} \quad \frac{55}{34} \quad \frac{89}{55} \quad = 1.618$$

$$(1.625) \quad (1.615) \quad (1.619) \quad (1.617) \quad (1.618)$$

* * * * * * * *

Derivatives of PHI:

$$\frac{1}{1.618} = .618 \qquad \sqrt{1.618} = 1.272 \qquad \sqrt{.618} = .786$$

Leonardo Fibonacci *(born 1179)*
During the Renaissance, Leonardo da Vinci used "the **Golden Proportion**" of PHI as the **Hermetic Framework** to create some of the great masterpieces.

© 2005 PHC, Fibonacci Series, The Future Healer

The derivation of the Fibonacci series

The Pyramid of Kukulcán, Chichen Itza

Glossary

Acupuncture—a technique for balancing the life-energy that travels along the acupuncture meridians. The meridian points, when out of balance, are either over or under-active, and typically must be stimulated or sedated to be brought back into harmony. Although the acupuncture points are classically treated with needles, some practitioners choose to use lasers, electrical stimulation or pressure to bring them back into balance.

Acupuncture meridians—the interconnected energy pathways for vital energy circulation throughout the body. The meridians link the emotional body with the physical, and may be used to affect emotional as well as physical conditions. To release the disruptions in the body's energy flow, specific points on the meridians, called acupoints, are stimulated via needles, pressure or other means.

Adonai—a Hebrew word, meaning "lord" or "ruler," bestowed upon God in the Old Testament.

Asana—Sanskrit for "seat", used to describe yoga postures, that help acquire concentration skills and assist with development of energetic structures of the body. Yoga postures are designed to create physical strength and flexibility, as well as to open spiritual energy centers in the subtle anatomies.

Astral Body—literally translates as "pertaining to the stars". The astral form is the subtle body connected to the heart chakra (IV), and associated with deep feelings of love. The heart chakra links the personal (chakras I, II and III) with the spiritual (chakras V, VI and VII), and is the point at which the human personality begins to take on its individual identity. Without the astral body, the mental and emotional would merge into the more impersonal levels of the causal and higher bodies, creating chaos in day-to-day consciousness as one became aware of the higher planes.

Atalon—a legendary ancient city that may have existed even before Lemuria.

Atlantis—an ancient continent, thought to have sunk into the ocean long before the beginning of recorded history. One of the hypotheses suggests that it is an Atlantean cult of technology that contributed to the eventual destruction of the Atlantean culture.

Aura—an energy field emanating from all living and many non-living objects. Separate layers of the aura are connected to form luminous multi-colored cocoons around the body. The existence of electromagnetic fields around objects can be demonstrated through Kirlian photography.

Bach flowers—vibrational remedies made from fresh flower petals, named after their creator, Edward Bach. Flower Remedies are often able to facilitate an emotional release in a patient. It is believed that this is because the flowers themselves are actually in resonance with the emotional level of one's energy field.

Blastema—a mass of undifferentiated cells capable of growth and regeneration into organs or body parts. A blastema is typically found in the early stages of development such as in embryos and in the regeneration of tissues, organs and bone.

Bodhisattva—an enlightened soul who delays his own final liberation in order to save all other beings out of his enormous compassion. He can rest and complete his own enlightenment only after accomplishing his mission to liberate others.

Brownian molecular motion—Robert Brown was an English botanist who, in 1827, first observed the constant movement of minute particles through his microscope. This movement came to be known as "Brownian Motion," after its discoverer, and eventually contributed to the scientific verification of the existence of molecules and atoms, which are constantly in motion on a microscopic level.

Capstone—the top of a pyramid, typically the upper one third, where the pyramidal energy becomes the most focused. The capstone of a pyramid is characteristically made of special materials, such as copper, gold, silver and quartz.

Causal Body—the energetic body associated with the power of the word, the throat chakra, and taking responsibility for our actions. It is here that sound creates and shapes matter. The causal level forms the pattern for the etheric body, which is, in turn, the energetic pattern for the physical.

Chakras—energy centers known as the "wheels of life" located along the spine. The seven major chakras correlate to seven planes of existence, as well as to seven levels of awareness and seven stages of personal development. They also act as lenses and vortices, focusing, transforming, and transmitting universal life force to maintain one's spiritual, mental, emotional and physical health in balance.

Chakras, higher—these are generally considered to be the fourth (heart), fifth (throat), sixth (brow), and seventh (crown) chakras, accordingly related to compassion, creative expression, spiritual vision and universal consciousness. These chakras give an individual the potential for spiritual awareness, while still maintaining a physical body.

Chakras, lower—considered to be the first (root), second (genital) and third (solar plexus) chakras, related to survival, reproduction and self-esteem. These chakras provide the potential for physical, emotional and mental focus, while still maintaining an essentially spiritual awareness.

Channel—someone able to receive messages from various levels of spirit. During *trance channeling*, the channel appears to have their consciousness leave the body to let a "source" enter. The channel's voice and mannerisms often change when the transition is complete. When the session is over, the trance channel again reconnects to their physical body.

Chiropractic—literally "to heal with the hands." Chiropractic is commonly considered to be a therapy that re-establishes healthy alignment of the spine, thereby allowing for normal nerve function from the brain to the organs and limbs. However, this definition can be expanded to include manipulation of the bones of the skull, extremities, internal organs and soft tissues of the body.

Christ Consciousness—consciousness existing as an invisible divine power and activating force that upholds all creation through vibration.

Color therapy—the use of color for the purpose of healing, based on the theory that various emotions, as well as points and regions of the body, resonate with different frequencies of light. In color therapy the seven rainbow colors correlate with the seven chakras, while the five colors of the Chinese acupuncture meridian system correlate with the Five Elements.

Corpus Callosum—a structure in the brain connecting the left and right cerebral hemispheres, appearing as a wide region of white matter located below the cortex. Much of the communication within the brain is carried over the corpus callosum.

Countenance of fellowship—the company of enlightened beings, or the fellowship of those who are seeking to grow in spiritual awareness.

De-differentiated cells—cells of the body that have reverted back to a more primitive unspecialized form, and may thus have the capacity to transform into almost any type of body cell, possibly leading to physical regeneration. The mechanisms for this process are not presently well understood. Though de-differentiation may lead to healing, in some cases it may also develop into certain types of malignant or cancerous cells.

Deva—a "being of light", or "shinning one" in Sanskrit. Also a term used to refer to a Hindu or Buddhist deity. Other connotations include a "celestial being of divine qualities", an "organizing intelligence of nature," and an "angelic being."

Device, the—see the **Pyramidal Device**

Dharma—the path of following one's spiritual destiny, leading to liberation. On the other hand, a life dictated by karma, or the momentum set in motion by one's previous actions, is said to keep an individual trapped on the wheel of birth and death.

Dharmic works—actions that are taken to fulfill one's spiritual path, therefore leading towards a greater awareness of the realms of light.

Divine conductor—the human physical body becomes increasingly able to act as a conduit for the higher forces as one grows in spiritual awareness. This transformation might also result in a greater capacity for self-regeneration.

Earth's chakras—similar to human beings, the Earth apparently has seven primary regions of energy focus that allow for the sustenance and transformation of the planet itself. These seven centers are further connected to seven locations in space, including the Seven Sisters, known in astronomy as *the Pleiades*.

Eighth chakra—a spiritual center located above the top of the head, said to integrate all of the seven chakras and to maintain a direct link with the higher self.

Elohim—a Hebrew word for God in the Bible. As there is no single way to describe Elohim, we can also be referring to a collective, who are essentially one with the Supreme Power, and are the co-creators of this, and perhaps other, universes.

Emotional Body—the vehicle through which we experience our feelings. This body contains all the colors of the rainbow, according to the type of emotions being experienced at the time, and corresponds to the second chakra. At this level, emotions are basically felt in relation to one's self.

Enoch—in the bible, Enoch is described as a direct descendant of Adam and an ancestor of Noah.

Etheric Body—the subtle body that is most directly associated with our physical form and is often called the *etheric double* because it precisely duplicates the physical body. It provides the energy for our awareness through the five senses and is associated with the first, or base, chakra that roots us to the physical plane. It provides us with physical energy and vitality and the experience of pleasure and pain. The ethereal level exists between the physical and emotional, and is where the acupuncture meridians are found.

Ethers, the—a universally pervading gas or energy that was hypothesized to exist in medieval times but was dismissed with the onset of science and the *Age of Reason*. The ethers are thought to be an energy that pervades all of creation, much like oxygen pervades the Earth's atmosphere. Ultimately, the ethers are thought to be the energetic foundation of the entire physical universe.

Expert Intuitive—someone highly skilled at tuning into a subject with the intuitive mind to gain information on an area of interest.

Faraday cage—a metal framework, first invented by the British physicist Michael Faraday in 1836, which totally surrounds a given space and screens out radio frequencies, creating a "quiet" electromagnetic environment. An automobile acts much like a Faraday cage if struck by lightning, protecting the passengers within.

Feminine consciousness—creative, loving, nurturing energy that is heart-based and involves the practice of love and compassion.

Fifth dimension—the level of energy that sustains the physical creation and keeps the universe in a continuous state of expansion, both literally and in consciousness. The fifth dimension is a subtle level of the ethers, and a part of the "yet to be discovered" laws of physics.

Fluidiums—the energetic fields surrounding a body, whether it is a human physical form or an entire planet.

Fourth dimension—the dimension comprising length, width, depth and *time*. This is the energetic level where the physical and ethereal bodies dwell. The fourth dimension is the normal time-space continuum and is governed by the laws of physics that the physical universe functions in.

Friend, the—in Biblical times, the Friend was known as Enoch. It was probably Enoch who, during a later time period on Earth, was ultimately responsible for the building of the Great Pyramid.

Futurism—foreseeing or anticipating what will take place in the future

Generator, the—see the **Pyramidal Device.**

Golden Mean—also **Golden Ratio** or **Golden Proportion**—See **Phi**

Homeopathy—from *homeo*, meaning same or similar, and *pathos*, meaning disease, homeopathy is the practice of using an infinitesimal amount of a substance to cure a disease, when a large dosage might cause that very same ailment. It is believed that homeopathic remedies stimulate a healing response by working in resonance with the various layers of the human energy field.

Homeworld—probably the origin of portions of humanity before people ever began the cycle of incarnation on Earth. The Pleiades and Orion are each a segment of Homeworld although it is not limited to one physical location, and apparently extends throughout many regions of space. One of its aspects is that all of the beings there are simultaneously aware of each other's existence, regardless of the plane of energy they exist upon.

Horticulture—from the Latin words *hortus* (garden plant) and *cultura* (culture), meaning "the culture of growing garden plants". Horticulturists work on improving crop yield, quality and nutritional value, and resistance to insects, diseases and environmental stresses.

Intuitive—*immediate* knowledge usually associated with the right hemisphere of the brain. When an individual works through the right hemisphere they first start with the *big picture* and then use the rational left hemisphere to *fill in the details*.

Kirlian photography—a photographic technology allowing for the visualization of an object's energy field, discovered by Semyon Kirlian in 1939. Kirlian photography introduces a high frequency, high voltage and ultra low amperage current into an object being photographed. As it travels through, this electrical energy makes the body's biological and energetic features visible. Kirlian photography also has the reputed ability to illuminate the acupuncture points of the human body.

Kundalini—a potential form of the life force, lying dormant in most individuals. Conceptualized as a serpent coiled up at the base of the spine, it can awaken spontaneously or when activated by spiritual practices. It originates in the first, or base chakra, but holds the potential to activate all of the spiritual centers as it rises up the spine.

Lemuria—sometimes referred to as the *continent of Mu*, or *the Motherland*, Lemuria was the original point of *grounding* of human life on Earth during mankind's descent from spirit into the physical plane. It is believed to have been an ancient civilization that began prior to the time of Atlantis. Lemuria was located in the South Pacific, somewhere between North America and Asia/Australia, and was probably the first Garden of Eden. All of its inhabitants existed at the same level of awareness, were connected telepathically, and shared equally in what was known as the planetary consciousness.

Ley-Lines—channels or conduits of energy that carry the life force upon the planet. They span the globe, traveling from pole to pole, much like the invisible acupuncture meridians that vitalize our physical bodies. In addition, just as we have major energy centers known as chakras, so too the Earth appears to have seven major energy centers that vitalize the entire planet.

Light and sound chamber—a domed structure containing a waterbed, lighting and sound system. It envelops an individual in sound, physical vibration and light, and is designed to create a healing environment for physical, emotional and spiritual transformation.

Magnetite—an iron oxide, Fe_3O_4, magnetite is a *ferromagnetic* substance produced in a crystalline form within certain portions of human and animal brains. Ferro-magnets are known for their ability to take on a strong magnetic charge, even when exposed to a relatively weak magnetic field. Magnetite may be directly responsible for the ability of certain animals, as well as some humans, to be consciously aware of various energetic fields, including changes in the Earth's electro-magnetic envelope.

Mandala—a geometrical pattern resonating with the universal life force, often enclosed within a circle. As tools for spiritual transformation, mandalas are said to open the energy centers in the subtle anatomies. Crop Circles, regardless of how they are made, are excellent examples of mandalas.

Meditation—the focusing and quieting of the mind. It has been said that prayer is talking to God, while meditation is listening for the answer.

Medulla oblongata—the lower portion of the brainstem that controls autonomic functions such as respiration and circulation and relays nerve signals between the brain and spinal cord. This is also the region that comprises part of the *primitive reptilian brain*, which is affected by our earliest, and often most deeply seated emotional experiences.

Melchizedek—in the Bible, Melchizedek was the anointer of Abraham, the founder of the Hebrew race, which eventually manifested Jesus. In modern times, Melchizedek is thought to remain in states of pure consciousness as one of the masters guiding the spiritual transformation of the planet. He might also be in communication with a hierarchy of beings associated with the Pleiades and Sirius.

Menders of karma—healers who are either empowered by their own connection with Spirit or are initiates of various masters, giving them the ability to mend the causal body of an individual, thus altering their karma, or destiny.

Mental Body—the vehicle of consciousness through which we experience the intellect and the ability to imagine and remember. The mental body deals with concrete thoughts and manifests primarily through the brain, spinal chord and solar plexus. It tends to have a yellow color, associated with the nervous system and mental activity.

Meridians—see **Acupuncture Meridians**

Multi-dimensional lives—the possibility that we are living all of our lives simultaneously. The fact that we perceive events as happening chronologically, one after another, may merely be the result of our limited fourth dimensional awareness in time and space.

Nadi—a channel for the life force that flows throughout the body. The *Ida* and *Pingala* are the two major nadis that wind around the *Shushumna,* the central channel in the spine that rises from the sacrum to the crown of the head. From these three primary conduits radiate the lesser channels, said to be 72,000 in all. The meridians may themselves be patterned after the *nadis,* which are a more intricate system of energy channels that exist on a subtler layer of our energetic anatomy.

Negative ions—negatively charged particles, created in nature, as air molecules break apart due to sunlight, radiation, and moving air and water. Negative ions increase the flow of oxygen to the brain and are believed to produce biochemical reactions that increase levels of the neurotransmitter serotonin, helping to alleviate depression, relieve stress, and boost energy.

Nubians—predecessors of the modern Egyptians, recorded in history as living about 5,000 years ago. It is likely, however, that they actually pre-date this time period.

Order of Melchizedek—a cosmic order of healers in consciousness. Led by Melchizedek, this group seeks to raise the spiritual awareness on the planet.

Phi—a number mathematically equal to 1.618, or its reciprocal, .618. Also known as the *Golden Ratio,* the *Golden Proportion* or the *Golden Mean,* Phi is a mathematical ratio that is found throughout nature, also showing up in great works of art and architecture. Phi is one of the most basic mathematical principals found in creation that allows for both natural and man-made physical forms to act in harmony with the creative forces of life.

Pi—the ratio of the diameter of a circle to its circumference, always equal to 3.1415....

Pineal gland—a small, pinecone-shaped structure located in the very center of the head. Some of the chemical substances produced by the pineal regulate the functions of other glands, including the pituitary, formerly believed to be the "master gland". It also produces major neuro-transmitters such as melatonin, serotonin and dopamine that, through their regulation of the brain, affect the entire body. The pineal controls the patterns of wakefulness and sleep, which are dependent on the level of melatonin secreted by the gland.

Pituitary gland—a gland located at the base of the brain beneath the hypothalamus, corresponding to the brow chakra, or *third eye*. Though there is evidence that it is regulated by the pineal, the pituitary is still generally known as the *master gland* because it controls most of the endocrine glands of the body. It manufactures many *trophic hormones* that in turn stimulate other hormone-producing glands, such as the thyroid, adrenals and gonads.

Piezo-electric—derived from the Greek *piezein,* which means to "squeeze" or "press", piezo-electric properties allow certain crystals to generate electricity when stimulated by pressure or vibration. Quartz crystals were originally the basis for early radios because of their piezo-electric ability to convert radio waves into electrical currents.

Planetary consciousness—the capacity for a *unified* awareness amongst all the inhabitants of the planet.

Planetary grid—the *energetic* grid-work of the Earth, which has its counterpart in the acupuncture meridian system of the human body.

Points of attunement—various points in space and on the Earth, along with specific points in our bodies, which are all connected together through resonance. It is via resonance, or *sympathetic vibration*, that the life force can be transmitted from one location to another.

Polarity Therapy—a healing system that works with the electromagnetic patterns of one's energy field expressed in mental, emotional and physical conditions. In some cases a practitioner might choose to use magnets, with their north and south poles, to balance one's energy field.

Points of leading and learning—physical locations on the planet that have been humanity's key points of spiritual development in the long history of the Earth.

Prana—a Sanskrit word meaning "breath," generally understood as the vital, universal force carried along the energy channels of the body.

Prodigal Son—from Luke 15 in the Bible, a wealthy son who squanders his inheritance, but finally is welcomed home by his loving and forgiving father.

Pyramid—see **Pyramidal Device**

Pyramidal Device—a project for spiritual and physical transformation, also called the **device**, the **pyramid** or the **generator**. A stainless steel pyramidal framework containing a single large crystal in the center and four crystal balls suspended above it, with the whole structure topped by a gold-plated capstone. The single crystal, with its seven energy centers, similar to man's seven chakras, naturally resonates with the planetary energy foci and the higher planes.

Rational—logical thought typically associated with the left, or *rational* side of the brain. When working with the rational, one first starts with the *details,* and then goes on to develop the *big picture* by adding the intuition.

Sacred Geometry—two or three-dimensional forms, that represent universal laws and principals of energy. They hold the potential to resonate with, and to conduct ethereal energies, which can affect our consciousness and subtle anatomies. Pyramids and spheres are two well-known examples of sacred geometry.

Science of light/Technology of light—science of the ethereal, which includes the study of the energetic make-up of the human form, such as the subtle bodies, chakras and meridians. This knowledge is then used to develop healing systems and technologies that promote wellbeing and personal transformation.

Seventh dimension—a plane of pure spirit associated with the seventh chakra and the universal mind.

Shambhala—a Sanskrit word meaning "place of peace, tranquility and happiness". In Tibetan Buddhist tradition, Shambhala was thought to be a mystical kingdom hidden somewhere in the Himalayan mountains. In modern usage, Shambhala typically refers to a state of awareness in those who have attained enlightenment.

Sixth dimension—a realm of pure consciousness, beyond the level of matter, time and space.

Soul group—souls that were created simultaneously in the cosmology, and therefore are likely to feel a deep and natural affinity for one-another.

Spirit guide—an ethereal being that leads a person on the path of spiritual unfoldment.

Spiritual Body—the body of light associated with universal love for all of life, corresponding to the sixth chakra.

Stem Cells—generally, cells which have not yet become *differentiated*, or *specialized*, and can remain *self-renewing* for many years. There are two different types of stem cells—*embryonic* and *adult*. In the embryo, the stem cells are the precursors for all of the cells that will eventually develop into the human form, whereas in an adult, they have the *potential* to become specialized cells.

Subtle anatomies/Subtle bodies—organized bodies of living energy that make-up an individual's energy field and precede the physical body, allowing for consciousness and the soul's expression on many levels.

Third dimension—the dimension defined by length, width and depth.

Trance channel—unlike an *intuitive channel,* that receives and communicates messages from non-physical realms while still remaining conscious, a trance channel is said to *leave his body* while another being temporarily comes in and speaks through him.

Tree of Knowledge—the spine with its seven chakras. As the kundalini force climbs like a serpent up the spinal column, it passes through, and awakens, the "seven seats of spiritual awareness". The term "knowledge" here refers to the various states of consciousness that are aroused by this awakening. In Gnostic Kabbalah the concept of the Tree of Knowledge is related to the study of Alchemy and Tantra.

Tree of Life—according to the Kabbalah, The Tree of Life is being, which represents the structure of the soul as the microcosm and the universe as the macrocosm. A tree of life in the form of ten interconnected nodes or the ten "luminous spheres of creation" is believed to also represent the spiritual centers in man.

Tulku—in Tibetan Buddhism, a tulku is an enlightened master, like the Dalai Lama, who has consciously decided to be reborn, often many times, to continue their spiritual pursuits. In other words, the reincarnation of a lama is seen as a continuation of the physical form of his predecessor, where the new incarnation is referred to as a tulku.

Universal Body—the body of light associated with divine mind and the seventh chakra, located at the crown of the head. This body forms a subtle egg-shaped energy field that encloses all the other bodies, and is the subtlest level of the aura. Through this body we can know that we are one with all.

Vibrational medicine—forms of treatment that have an energetic versus a physical basis.

Yoga—meaning "union with God", yoga is a system of ancient spiritual practices originating in India, and one of the six schools of Hindu philosophy. Outside India, yoga has become primarily associated with the asanas, or postures, of hatha yoga—a system of physical culture that was developed to prepare students for the practice of meditation.

Bibliography

Malvin N. Artley, Jr., *Bodies of Fire* (Jersey City Heights, NJ, University of the Seven Rays Publishing House, 1992)

Robert Becker, MD, *The Body Electric—Electromagnetism and the Foundation of Life* (New York, NY, Quill Publishers, 1987)

The Bhagavad-Gita (Hollywood, California, Vedanta Press, 1969)

Sushila Blackman, *Graceful Exits* (Shambhala, 2005)

Barbara Brennan, *Hands of Light, A Guide to Healing Through the Human Energy Field* (New York, NY: Bantam Books, 1987)

Gabriel Cousens, MD, *Spiritual Nutrition and the Rainbow Diet* (North Atlantic Books, 2004)

Dhammapada—the Path of Dharma, a Buddhist text

John Diamond, MD, *Life Energy: Using the Meridians to Unlock the Hidden Power of Your Emotions* (Creativity Publishing, 1992)

Gyorgy Doczi, *The Power of Limits* (Boston, MA, Shambhala, 1994)

Kerry Emanuel, *Divine Wind: The History and Science of Hurricanes* (Oxford University Press, 2005)

Patrick Flanagan, *Pyramid Power* (Earthpulse, 1997 reprint)

Richard Gerber, MD, Vibrational Medicine—New Choices for Healing Ourselves (Sante Fe, NM, Bear & Co., 1988)

James Hurtak, The Keys of Enoch (Los Gatos, CA, Academy for Future Science, 1977)

Brugh Joy, Joy's Way (Jeremy Tarcher, 1979)

William Kautz, Channeling: The Intuitive Connection (San Francisco, Harper and Row, 1987)

Elizabeth Kubler-Ross, The Wheel of Life (New York, NY, Scribner, 1977)

Peter Lemesurier, The Great Pyramid Decoded (Great Britain, Element Books, 1987)

Jacob Liberman O.D., Ph.D., Light—Medicine of the Future (Sante Fe, NM, Bear & Co., 1991)

Bruce Lipton, The Biology of Belief (Mountain of Love, 2005)

Shirley MacLaine, Out on a Limb (Bantam Books, 1984)

Dean Ornish, Dr. Dean Ornish's Program for Reversing Heart Disease (Ballantine, 1991)

Rig Vedas—In Praise of Knowledge, a collection of Vedic Sanskrit hymns

Pat Rodegast, Emmanuel (New York, NY, Bantam Books, 1985)

Kevin Ryerson, Spirit Communication: The Souls Path (Bantam Books, 1991)

Jason Serinus, Psychoimmunity—Key to the Healing Process (Celestial Arts, 1986)

Nikola Tesla, Colorado Springs Notes (Belgrade, Yugoslavia, Nolit, 1978)

Peter Tomkins, *Secrets of the Great Pyramid* (New York, NY, Harper & Row, 1971)

Lao Tsu, *Tao Te Ching* (New York, NY, Vintage Books, 1989)

George Vithoulkas, *The Science of Homeopathy* (Athens, Greece, George Vithoulkas, 1978)

Neale Donald Walsch, *Conversations with God* (New York, NY, Putnam, 1996)

Brian Weiss, *Messages from the Masters* (New York, NY, Warner Books, 2000)

Paramahansa Yogananda, *Autobiography of a Yogi* (Los Angeles, California, Self Realization Fellowship, 1979)

978-0-595-40825-2
0-595-40825-7

Printed in the United States
113246LV00004B/141/A